We were, and stil.
longer fight in distant wars, or look down the scope of a weapon to see a little red dot dancing on the temple of Mr. Unlucky. We do not wear fatigues, nor do we report to a higher command (unless you're married or have children). Nor do we make every merciful attempt to not fall victim to another onslaught of the evil and torturous PowerPoint presentation.

We've gained a few pounds, grown beards and mustaches that the gods of Valhalla themselves would look down upon and smile in admiration. We relive our glory days with our brothers and sisters of war as we toss back cheap bottles of beer and whiskey, laughing as we are reminded of our close encounters with death. We are made somber to the thoughts of those that were not fast enough to escape the call of the almighty. We have given much in service and have returned, different and empty. Somewhere on the battlefield are the remnants of our souls, childhood, hopes, love and motivation. Yet, we did not return home empty handed. A few metal pieces are pinned to our chest that we wear with pride. A few ribbons, colorful and bright that demand the respect from your fellow man. You've gained experience, but with it came misunderstanding. Confidence and confusion. Remorse and ambivalence. Pride and pain. Sorrow and anger.

This work, I dedicate to you, brothers and sisters of war. Those who I've fought with side by side, held in pain and agony; those to whom I have raised my cup and shared bread with. To those that will never understand what it is to be a part of such an exclusive club, it's not your fault—the price is just too high to join.

I'm not a doctor, nor am I a psychiatrist. What I am is broken. I am the one that struggles to put these shattered pieces back together, and in the process, I have learned to cope with the pain and anger that most likely lives within you too. As the great General Sun Tzu stated in his book, *The Art of War*, "If you know the enemy and know yourself, you need not fear the result of a hundred battles." Anger is my enemy, and I know him well. I'd wager that if you are a veteran, there is no need for an introduction as I'm sure you have a very well established relationship too. You know the kind of anger, the subtle, boiling anger that turns your blood to lava. The itchy neck that needs to be ripped from your flesh. The kind of anger that makes you reach to a higher power because you hope and pray that this won't be the moment that judges what path your life takes. My hope is that I can help you choose a different path, a path that doesn't involve so much anger. A path that allows for healthy relationships and peace. A path that allows you to help others find the raging fire that burns from within, and for once, extinguish the flame, or at the very least bring the fervor down to a dull simmer. It is time to let go of the fear and anger. It's time to push pass our sorrows and pain, to allow ourselves to grow and heal. You've held on to it for far too long.

If you're not a veteran, I commend you on reading this book. There are many veterans that never give an outsider the chance to understand our anger. We become mute, insulted at the simple question of our time in war. It's not your fault, we're really not mad at you. We're just angry. Hopefully, you will find the answers you are searching for. Hopefully, one day, you might be able to understand. Even if you don't and never will, I thank you for trying. It shows that you truly do care, and that means the world to me, to us.

Disclaimer:

Please be aware that there will be very graphic descriptive content in this book. Some of the graphic content is focused on fallen warriors. I describe these scenes in full and visual detail to help you, the reader, try and understand what I saw and experienced. This is in no way shape or form meant to dishonor or disrespect my fellow brothers and sisters in arms who have made the ultimate sacrifice. I want you to see what I saw and feel what I felt. This may help you understand what myself and other countless veterans have gone through. For those who have lost loved ones in war, I offer my deepest condolences.

Sign me up!

There are two dates you never forget when you join the military: your enlistment date and your ETS (Expiration of Term of Service). October 9, 2002 was the day I swore an oath to protect my country, from all enemies, foreign and domestic. God, that was so long ago—I was only 17 and a half. If you would have asked me then if I would have ever thought about joining the military, I would have said no, I was going to go to college. Well, things don't always work out the way we plan. As I write this book, I have three finals to prepare for that will bring me one step closer to graduating with a bachelor's in business administration. I'm 33 years old.

So, how did I end up joining the military? Well, two main reason reasons that were heavily influenced by one man: my father.

You see, my father, as a young boy, always wanted to join the Peruvian Marines. I think it was his affinity for the water (he was a competitive swimmer in his heyday) and the military. Now, the military in Peru works a little differently than in the US, as I found out on my last trip there. In Peru, the military is a special club that's very hard to get into. Usually, you need to have a sponsor referred to as a "padrino" (godfather) that gets you in. I've been told the Peruvian military doesn't pay much, but it has its perks—paid training and education (which are relatively expensive in Peru), steady pay checks, you get to live on base, social status, and there are rumors of Peruvian military receiving free gas. Granted, by American standards, these are all very basic requirements when caring for your troops. (Although, free gas would be greatly appreciated.)

Alas, it would not be the lack of connections that would deny my father his entry into the Peruvian military, but something just as bad. It was his health. At a young age, my father contracted tuberculosis, and with it his dreams of joining the Peruvian military, sailing across the open seas, and serving his country came to an abrupt halt. His dream was never meant to be, but maybe, it could live on through someone else.

As a child, I can remember my father always encouraging me to join the United States Army because it would, as he said, make a man out of me. He was certain that it would give me a great future and ability to get ahead in life. He was right, in part. Yet, I only saw myself going to university, getting a "good job," and living a simple and happy life. Might I remind you, I'm 33 and still working on that bachelor's. Many of my old high school friends have already completed their education, been married, have children, and have spent years in their respective career fields. They got the good job and the simple life.

I never really thought about joining the military until I realized, "How the hell am I going to pay for school?" I knew my family didn't have any money to send me to college and grants would only help so much. So, what could I do?

(Cue the knock at the door.)

Knock, knock.

There he stood, back straight, tall, lanky build of a man, pressed green BDUs, black boots that could reflect the sun, your soul, and an angel's halo. He had high and tight (it was all the rave when I was in) gold rimmed spectacles, a thin mustache, and that used car salesman smile. My savior from college debt, my deliverance from ramen noodles, my army recruiter.

Like any good salesman, your recruiter will promise you the moon, the stars, and his undivided love and attention; for the small, one-time fee of your fucking soul. Damn, that's a tall price, but man, that college thing sounds pretty sweet. You can just see the recruiter now:

"Yup!" says the recruiter as he slaps the hood of the college degree. "This baby can be all yours. You just gotta sign the dotted line, champ. It's gonna be great, trust me."

I took some time to think it over ... really think it over. Like any good salesman, they keep your focus on the shiny lights; they don't let you worry about all that other stuff. You know, war stuff. Some recruiters will make it seem like you're going to summer camp and you'll be back home eating ma's home cooking in no time.

I started to think about my future, going to college, earning my degree, getting that good job. Then I thought about my parents. What would they have done if given this opportunity? They encouraged me to take it, but I still wondered, would they have done the same? My parents could never be given an option like this because they weren't born in the United States. They came to the US illegally. It was extremely hard for my parents when they first arrived here. They met on a farm, picking cabbages, 12 hours a day, 6–7 days a week. They took any job that would bring them any kind of income. They scraped by for years before being able to live a better life for themselves and their children. I wouldn't have to do any of that. I was an American-born citizen. I could go to public school, receive financial aid or loans even. I didn't have to get paid under the table, didn't have to worry about immigration and deal with threatening bosses. Yet, for many years, my parents didn't have any rights. The only difference between my parents and I was that, when I was born, I hit American soil, they didn't. Knowing what my parents and many others like them endured when they first came to this country, I felt grateful for all the opportunities America had and would provide me. I felt I owed my parents and country for all that I had. Lastly, there was one more influencing factor that would push me to join the military. I was 16 when I saw the second tower come crumbling down on TV. Nothing like that had ever happened to our country, and it felt as if we had been sucker punched. I'll never forget the images of the second plane crashing into the building, seeing people jump out of the windows because they didn't want to be burned alive. 9/11 had changed America and it had changed me as well.

I signed the dotted line.

Like the majority of other veterans, I had no idea what the hell I was doing, nor could I have known the path that I had just placed myself on. To be honest, I thought I would be going to summer camp and would be back home in time to start classes at CSUF. However, the military has a very funny and humbling way of letting you know that you don't know your ass from your elbow.

It was all fun and games on the flight to basic training. I made some friends on the flight; we were all laughing, joking around. It was great! Fort Jackson, South Carolina would be where I would call home for the next nine weeks of my life. My recruiters gave me high hopes about the place. They called it, "Relaxing Jackson"! They told me how lucky I was and that it would be a walk in the park. I thought I was really lucky to go to such a fun basic training.

The jokes continued at the airport and on the bus to Fort Jackson. Everyone was all smiles and having a grand time. I don't think any us of really noticed that we had left the city and were on an open highway. I don't remember it getting dark. but all of a sudden, I noticed it was pitch black as we continued on our journey on a desolate road. One by one, everyone started to realize the same thing—there was nothing around us, and it was dark. Too dark. No highway lights, no city lights, nothing. You could feel the tension building.

In the distance, there was a small glimmer of light, and as we made our way closer, we could start to make out a very large gate beside a small office. Nobody was talking at this point; no more laughing, no more joking, just an eerie silence. I looked in the rear view mirror and locked eyes with the soldier driving the bus. He looked back at me and a single smirk escaped his stone like face. Something didn't feel right.

We finally approached the gate. The guard exchanged some words and documents with the driver, and a minute later, the bus started back up again. That's when we heard it. The long dying screech of a rusted, iron gate opening. The gate howled a warning to us, begging us not to enter, but it was too late. With its final screech it proceeded to close us off from the rest of society. A thunderous clank echoed through the night as it shut. That's when it dawned on me. I wasn't going to summer camp. It was this moment I started to question my life decision.

A few more miles down the road we stopped at a building that was low lit with yellow tinted lights. The driver calmly turned off the engine and exited the bus. We weren't sure if we should follow him but didn't have time to even ponder the idea once "he" boarded the bus.

He stood there, tall, rigid with a square jaw. We couldn't see his eyes because the brim of his hat covered them. He wore a green camouflaged uniform, black polished boots, and his sleeves were rolled up, exposing a set of very wide forearms. He balled his fists ever so tight.

"I want all you pieces of shit off my bus in 30 motherfucking seconds!" the drill sergeant yelled.

Without hesitation, everyone grabbed their bags and got off the bus as quick as humanly possible. Everyone was confused and scared, and at that moment, the others came out from the shadows. Shark attack! A swarm of drill sergeants fell upon us like ninjas and yelled conflicting commands within inches of our faces.

"Pick up that bag, private!" "I thought I told you to put that bag down, private!" "Tuck in that doggone shirt!" "You eyeing me, private!?" "Oh, so you think you special!?" "Look at this private, he must think he's back on the block!" "Did I give you permission to speak!?" "Why are you still standing here!?" "Move with a purpose, private!"

I started to realize that my recruiters might have lied to me about Fort Jackson. Actually, they might have lied about a few other things, too.

How an Angry Veteran is Made

We all have a part of our military career that has given birth to the angry veteran inside of us. This persona was carved out from the darkest corners of our souls, and through the horrors of war manifested into a part of us that will stay with us forever. Where did you first meet your angry veteran? Was it in the trenches of Germany? The beaches of Normandy? The Pusan perimeter? The jungles of Vietnam? The sand dunes of Kuwait? Or were you like me and found your other self in a shit FOB at the Pakistani border?

FOB Salerno, aka "Rocket City," Khost, Afghanistan.

My home away from home.

2008 would be the year I geared up to go to Afghanistan. However, I didn't really know I would be going. I was slotted as a tertiary back up to the other two knuckle draggers (in case they fucked up and couldn't go to war). Turns out, they fucked up. Well to be fair, one of them fucked up so bad that it landed his ass in jail. The other—Mr. Hooah, lock and load, battle ready mother fucker—well, poor guy couldn't go 'cause his knees hurt. I'm sure a few of you reading knew of someone just like this. It always seems to be the loudest of heroes who drops out before his card is pulled and lucky bastards like me get to go in their place. I should have been playing the lottery with my luck.

I was voluntold to be the NCOIC of the patient administration division (PAD). I was an E-5 Sergeant, in an E-7 Sergeant First Class slot (go fucking figure) and worked with one other E-5 sergeant, SGT. C. Together we were the ones who kept the gears turning in our little PAD office. PAD to the Bone!

We had both come from a combat support hospital (CSH) unit in Los Angeles, CA, the 349th CSH. We were attached to the 101st Airborne Division ("Screaming Eagles") under the 506th Infantry Regiment ("Currahee"). I must admit, it was pretty amazing and inspiring to be supporting such a prestigious and time honored unit such as the 101. I adorned my 101 patch on my right shoulder and wore it with pride, but my new unit, the 349th, wasn't as prestigious as the 101st.

The 349th CSH was a bunch of weekend warriors from LA. We weren't the most squared-away bunch; half of the officers didn't know shit about basic uniform etiquette or soldiering skills and the junior enlisted were always off dicking around. Hell, being reservists and in the medical field made us the military equivalent of redheaded stepkids. We got a lot of the shit details and hand-me-down equipment (we deployed to Afghanistan with M16s in 2008). A majority of the junior enlisted skated out of duty or training by disappearing into supply cages to catch some z's. Sham-shielders for life was our motto and I'd be lying if I said I didn't wear the shield. You probably did too at some point. A lot of us were just lost in the sauce when we were back in the rear. AT and drill mostly consisted of getting shitface drunk, fights, and arrests, but man, when we were deployed we were pretty fucking awesome. As disgruntled and nonchalant as we were, when it came to deployments, we were high speed.

We had the added experience that most of the soldiers in the 349th were working professionals in their respective medical fields. Doctors, nurses, X-ray techs, lab-techs, patient admins, surgical techs and many others. We did our jobs on a daily basis where at times, active duty wouldn't get that same consistent training. So when it came to showing up and doing the job, we excelled and left the active duty soldiers flabbergasted. They would be amazed that reservists could work so well and would give us compliments such as, "Wow, for being reservists you guys aren't that bad." We've earned a few unit ribbon awards. No biggie.

Now an attachment of this same ragtag bunch of military misfits would be joining the ranks of the 101st. We wanted to make our unit proud, to make other reservists proud and to prove that we were just as capable as our full-time brethren. We sure as hell did, but we all paid a price for that respect—we had to leave a little bit of ourselves in Afghanistan to walk among giants.

But there's a funny question that comes up often when people find out that I served in Afghanistan: "How was it?" I always respond with the same answer. "It was the best and worst times of my life".

It really was and nothing could have prepared me for what I would encounter. All the training, pep talks, Power Point slides, booze, and pussy could never prepare you for war. Yet, I wasn't the guy pulling the trigger. I was just some Fobbit, working as a patient administration specialist. What could I have seen?

Things I pray no one else has to see.

When describing war, we don't really focus on all the good parts of war (yes, there are some good parts to it). Why don't we? The more haunting moments of war run deeper than the good ones. The bad times change us, but the good times help us deal with the physical and emotional anguish that comes with war. Some of the best memories I have in Afghanistan were on top of a flight deck, drinking near-beer, smoking stogies, and watching the Black Hawks and AC-130s take off as we bitched and complained about the day we had just had. Those were the best nights, where enlisted officers put aside ranks, creeds, and differences all in a harmonious effort to vent about everything and anything that could have gone wrong. It was very therapeutic. We'd laugh, talk shit, and say things like, "What a fucking day. They don't know what the fuck they're doing. Are they fucking serious!? Are you fucking serious!? I can't wait to get the fuck outta here. Just three more fucking months."

It still makes me smile to think of these moments. It makes me miss them all, and I'm grateful that I was there with them and not anybody else.

It's the scary times that you realize how much you need each other, how much you are all alike, how you can laugh off anything you go through.

So no shit, there I was, lying in bed, dead asleep after a long day of exploring the base, meeting the chain of command, getting to know where the DFAC was, the bazaar, a small restaurant named "Aziz's" which had the best cinnamon naan. There was even a goat that was the base mascot. The goat ate like a king because everyone would stop by to pet him and give him food. It was a lot to take in. Needless to say, I was exhausted on my first day in the sandbox.

Boom! I was then violently awakened by explosions. I didn't know what the hell was going on but soon realized we were being hit with incoming rounds. I shared a brick and mortar with eight other guys and we all knew we were awake. More shelling, more explosions... we were all scared shitless, and everyone knew it. Protocol was to stay under cover during mortar attacks. We could hear the artillery boys returning fire and just dumping on the enemy with a hail storm of American-made cannisters of freedom. Get some.

After a few minutes of exchange, the explosions stopped. "Attention on the FOB, attention on the FOB, all clear, all clear." It was safe now, yet it was eerily quiet. You could hear a scorpion fart it was so damn quiet, but we knew we were all awake. We were trying to process what had just happened and realized we just survived our first attack. Then, out of nowhere, SGT. Y yells, "Who's going to check on the goat?" We all burst out laughing. We all denied being afraid and started calling each other scared little bitches. It turned into a big shit talking event for half an hour as we judged each other's manhood and debated who was the weaker one of the group. The homoerotic calls were strong that night. After some laughs and crude insults, one by one we fell asleep. Afghanistan had properly welcomed us home that night.

P.S. The goat made it.

I can laugh at these stories now. I can reminisce about these fun-filled events that made war a little bit more livable. However, let me remind you, this isn't one of the stories that changed me. This was one of the moments that helped get me through some of the worst times. Everyone who has been to war has a particular story, an event that shattered a little bit of themselves. One or many particular events would change how veterans feel and see the world. For some veterans, it's seeing the lifeless bloody body of a their best friend, or the charred remains of the driver that died because of an IED explosion.

You can never forget the look and smell of a burnt corpse. I know this too well. I once received the body of a soldier, still hot to the touch. His unit had been on the way home having just finished their tour and they were coming around the corner of the local village to get to our base, to go home. That's when the Humvee was hit with an RPG. There were five passengers if I recall correctly—driver, passenger, gunner, and rear passengers. I think only one survived that day but he lost an arm. Luckily, they recovered his arm and I was able to retrieve his wedding band and watch.

The smell of burnt flesh will never, ever leave your memory. It's like burnt hair and blood, a fowl, potent smell mixed with the scent of charcoal. The poor soldier had been burnt so bad that you could barely tell he was once human. His bones were blackened, radio gear melted to his shoulders and neck. Everything was black—his liver, intestines, spleen, everything. His skull was powdered black with very little tissue left. It was so gruesome it looked fake. I can't watch slasher movies to this day because of what I saw. He was so close to joining all his buddies in going home to their family and friends. Instead, he would be going home in a box. It frustrated me to think about this, and it angered his comrades to know that they were just around the corner to going home, everyone intact. Their unit had had no casualties up until that point. It's a pretty fucked up joke if you ask me. It hurt a lot to see his friends in so much pain, but it wasn't the first time I saw soldiers mourn the loss of a fellow brother and it wouldn't be the last time. It sucked every time. I hated being the one to tell them their buddy didn't make it. I hated preventing them from seeing their friend's body but I didn't want them to have the last image of their friend be this disfigured pile of burnt flesh and bones. Remember the man as he was. I never thought I would have to see these kinds of things. After all, I was chairborne ranger, pencil-pushing son of a bitch working in the safety of hospitals. Yet, here I was, trying to comfort soldiers while trying move the bodies of fallen heroes.

The death of a soldier always brought reflection, pain, anger, and sorrow. We had saved a lot of soldiers but we weren't able to save them all. It was really a mixed bag of emotions for us every time we lost one. No time for jokes, no time for high fives or shit talking. I just felt exhausted and tired, depressed even. There were very few things that could really hit me like the death of the soldier, but kids were a different story.

I love kids, I always have. I'm the eldest of four, so I've always had a soft spot for kids. I think we all do really. Children are innocent, pure, loving, and can bring so much joy to the world. Have you ever had a whiff of that brand new baby smell? It's better than new car smell. So whenever I encountered children amidst the war, I always perked up. We would see lots of children; I believe it was Tuesdays that we had an open clinic for families and children. They would come in to get treated for injuries or illnesses and we'd give them some medical supplies. One of my duties was to speak some Pashtun (the Afghani language of the Pashtun people), translate, triage, and do background checks on all LNs (local nationals). I was able to meet a lot of the Afghani people and kids. They were grateful that we were providing aid to them. The local hospital didn't have enough supplies or equipment to meet the needs of the people so we helped where we could. I know it was all part of winning the hearts and minds of the people but I really liked helping the local people. I could see that you were having a positive impact on someone's life and it made me feel good about what I was doing there.

Before being mobilized to Afghanistan, I was working part-time at the Disneyland resort as a valet attendant for the Paradise Pier hotel. My managers knew I was in Afghanistan, and when I brought up the idea of donating to the children of Afghanistan, they jumped at the opportunity. I don't know who they contacted from Disney headquarters but I was getting all sorts boxes of clothes, toys, and other Disney merchandise. It was really nice to see that Disney was trying to spread a little Mickey joy to these kids in a war-torn country. I have a little confession to make—whenever Disney sent me "princess" dresses, I always saved the best for my very own princess, Asman.

Asman had to be the most beautiful and sweetest nine year old girl in Afghanistan. She was full of light and happiness in a very dark and dangerous world. I met her when her father came into the clinic to have reconstructive surgery for his foot. He had stepped on a landmine, and by some miracle didn't lose his foot. Asman had these huge brown eyes that melted your heart, a soft smile, a green gem pierced to the side of her nose, and she was always well-groomed and presentable. Her father took very good care of her. She greeted everyone with a hug and a smile. She shattered the icy walls from the toughest soldiers. There was no way you could see this little angel and not be happy to see her. Whenever Asman's father would come to the clinic, she would hang out with me in my office. We'd draw, practice writing our Arabic numbers, and try to have conversations with my limited Pashtun. This became a regular routine for us, to the point where all the other soldiers would call her my "Afghani princess." She sure was. At the time, I was dating an Afghan girl back home and had a picture of her on my desk. Asman was drawn to the picture and I could tell she was curious about who this woman was. She pointed and I assumed she asked, "Who is she?" Since Afghans, at least at the time, don't date, I didn't know how to tell her she was my girlfriend. So I pointed at the picture and said, "Afghani, khaza," trying to tell her that the woman in the picture was Afghan and my wife. Her eyes lit up and she was very excited. She must have thought it was so strange and interesting for this foreign man to have married an Afghan woman. My girlfriend even had the opportunity to talk to Asman over the phone once. Asman was very excited and happy to have met my "wife."

I was lucky enough to see Asman one last time. I was on tower guard duty as her and her father came into for his final checkup. It seems as though he was fully recovered and would no longer need further care. Since everyone in the hospital knew that Asman and I had developed a special bond during her visits; a buddy of mine came to relieve me so that I could say my goodbyes. It was really nice of him to do that for me. I raced across the base to get to the hospital wearing my full battle rattle in hopes that I would be able to see my friend, one last time.

I made it to the clinic side of the hospital in the nick of time. Her father was gathering his belongings and was receiving final care instructions from the doctor and terp. Asman lit up when she saw me and made her way to me. She gave me a strong and loving hug and said everything she needed to say with one look and a smile. It's as if she told me she was happy to have met me. I was very happy to have had the chance to say goodbye to my little Afghani princess. As a parting present, she removed one of her rings and gave it to me. I tried to refuse but she insisted and I had a very hard time saying no to her. My buddies all joked around that I had just got married and had better not let my girl back home know. She gave me one last hug, we took our last picture together, and I haven't seen her since.

I miss her sometimes. I worry about her a lot. She'd be about 19 now. I wonder how her life turned out. Did she survive the war? Did she continue her studies, start a career, settle down and have a family? It's crazy how someone can have such an impact on your life that you still think about them and remember every detail about them. I used to have dreams about Asman. Even if I never see her again, I hope she is well and happy. That would be the greatest news. I still get emotional when I talk about her. She was a shining light in a very dark time of my life and made the war just a little bit more bearable.

I'm sure the majority of you veterans have met your very own Asman. There was someone, something that showed you a different side of war. One that made you think and feel, "Today won't be so bad." As much Asman filled my heart with joy, there was another little angel that melted my heart and gave me joy while in Afghanistan. Her name is Faridah.

I first met Faridah as she was being carried into our emergency room. She came from a different region of the country, and was being treated for second and third degree burns. The story we were told was that she fell into a cooking fire; we all knew that was fat lie. We later found out more details about what more likely happened, and that seemed to make more sense after seeing her injuries. Terps told us that there were cases of children being beaten, burned, or injured in order to persuade their parents to not help coalition forces. In some cases, babies would be dipped into boiling pots. Faridah had sustained second and third degree burns from the bottoms of her feet, legs, pubic area, buttocks, and lower back. She was covered in boils. Faridah was less than a year old.

The first week was very intense for her, from the horrible injuries she sustained, having no family members with her, surrounded by people she could not recognize nor understand in the least. We looked different, smelled different, the environment (military hospital) was completely different than what she may have been used to. This child was transplanted in a different world with life-threatening injuries. Now, we were charged to be her healers, caretakers, teachers, and parents.

We were angry. Fuming mad. Pissed off to high heaven. Not that we were now responsible for the life of this child, but that any human would be capable of such an atrocity. Actually, no animal would have done something like this. Only a fucking monster, a demon who would sink to the very dark corners of their soul and think this was acceptable. We didn't know the child but our hearts ached for her. It was as if we felt someone was doing this to our own child. We'd kill the son of a bitch if we ever got our hands on him, have him take a dip in boiling water and make him regret the day he ever thought of hurting this child.

Faridah would need round the clock care and was assigned a nurse to be her main caretaker. SGT. L would be with her every second he was able to. There were other nurses and medics that would help and rotate care as well but we all knew that was SGT. L's baby, we were just happy to have her in our lives too.

With the severity of Faridah's injuries she would need constant bandage changes, creams applied, and skin grafts. So, operation chubby baby was started. She ate and ate and ate. We got her to be chunky little thing. One of her favorites meals, which was also beneficial in getting her nice and plump, was mayo, potatoes, milk, and butter all mixed together. I bet if half of you ate this your ass would jiggle for a week. (Don't forget, PT is free.)

By this point, Faridah had become used to us soldiers. On the long nights where everyone was busy and I was done with my duties, I'd help out the nurses and medics with Faridah. If anything, to just give them a break to stretch their legs, get some chow, or have a smoke. Faridah loved to be carried around for walks and meet other people. I think everyone was just as happy to meet her. She sparked a bit of joy in everyone's day/night. At times, I'd hang out with her at the nurse's station and sing her the same Spanish lullabies my parents sang to me. She seemed to enjoy them, or maybe it was the goofy faces I made. I was just glad to see her smile and giggle. She also had a knack for trying to bite my lips and nose. She would also grab my cheeks and just stare at me, trying to understand me or figure me out. It warmed my heart. To think, we were in the middle of a war and I had the luxury of hearing a baby laugh. To hold her, play with her, see her, and smell her. I would block everything else out and for a moment, I was happy. Then came the day she had to leave.

She was all healed up now. Her mother had come down to retrieve her and she was getting ready to fly back to her village via Black Hawk. We were all saying our goodbyes with hugs, kisses, and pinched cheeks. Before the day, SGT. C, my counterpart, had collected all the pictures we had of her and made a slideshow of all the pictures. Some were of her smiling, sitting by herself with her crazy hair sticking straight up. There was even a picture of her with one of our officers rocking the same side-swept receding hairline look. There were lots of pictures of her with other soldiers and in every picture you can see the happiness pouring out of us. We held her, raised her, and loved her as our own daughter. Imagine, a group of 30 or so combat soldiers raising one baby girl? We're supposed to be physically and mentally tough, but you would have seen a group of battle tested soldiers sobbing like little kids at the thought of us having to give our baby back. We didn't want to. All of us wanted to adopt her and bring her home but it wasn't our place. She left us and took a piece of our hearts with her.

It still hurts. It hurts so damn much that I have a hard time holding back my tears now. We weren't prepared to deal with these emotions. There was nothing about baby raising in the Power Point slides that taught us how to properly go to war. God, I miss her and I hope she is well. Faridah would be about 10 years old today.

I never realized how much Faridah and Asman would impact me until years later as I sat in a psychiatrist's office at the VA hospital. I was asked to describe the more traumatic points of my time in Afghanistan. I spoke of Asman and Faridah and broke down in tears. I felt every pent-up feeling I ever had of them pouring out. I had recently been going through a break up, and the woman I was in a relationship had a daughter. I truly loved her little girl, and losing her while talking about Asman and Faridah was too much to handle. It's crazy how our emotions connect the dots, even when we aren't aware of them. At the time, I couldn't even understand why I was crying talking about Faridah and Asman, but now I do. Sometimes, it takes years for us to realize the storm that lies beneath our surface.

My time in Afghanistan only had two settings: non-stop or nothing. When there was nothing going on, we begged the battle gods to send us something to do. Give us something to shoot, someone to patch up, someone to train... something! We would die of boredom before we were hit with shells. Want to know why so many vets come back swoll as shit? Sometimes the gym is all they have to do, and you might work out two to three times a day because there is nothing else to do. One of the guys in our unit had bought an Xbox 360 and it was a godsend. At times where there was nothing to do, we'd continue our training with *Call of Duty* or *Gears of War*. Things got really interesting when a second person bought another Xbox 360. People still hold grudges to this day over those games. However, videogames could only keep us at ease for so long, and when the real fun started, it was a non-stop roller coaster ride to hell.

Depending on the number of TICs (troops in combat) that were going on in our area, we could determine how busy we would be. The more TICs, the more patients we would receive and the more work we had to look forward to. Sadly, it wasn't always just soldiers we would receive in our emergency room. Whenever there was combat, there were almost always civilian casualties. One such firefight led to the death of an eight year old little boy. Soldiers had exchanged fire with the enemy and young boy had somehow been caught in the middle of it. He may have ran through the middle of the fighting and was shot in the thigh. Unfortunately, the bullet severed his femoral artery. A soldier applied a tourniquet but the kid was so skinny that when I received the child, he had already bled out. The tourniquet was too lose and couldn't stop the bleeding. This boy would be the first child I would have to put into a box. This is one of the pivotal moments that broke me.

Out of everything you can see in war, a dead kid is something you never want to see. It's too heartbreaking and hard to wrap your head around. You're not supposed to see dead kids. It's not supposed to happen, but it did. I carried the kid onto the table of the mortuary affairs. We had a terp come in to conduct prayers and tend to the body. I helped with what I could. We tied the boys thumbs and toes together, then the jaw. The terp said a few prayers over him and I just stayed quiet and watched. It didn't look like it was the terp's first time doing this. I think I was in shock but unable to understand the feelings that I had. After the prayer, the terp began cleaning thy boy's body. I felt it only right I help too. I guess I thought it would have been rude or disrespectful if I didn't help. I'm glad I helped, at least I was able to show I cared. You don't have to understand someone's culture or religion to care. After the boy was cleaned up, I moved his body to the freezer. We reached out to the local hospital in Khost and arranged a pick up of the boy. From there, they would try to find the boy's family and have the remains collected. However, with no IDs, not everyone having a cellphone, and no real infrastructure, reuniting with loved ones or the deceased would prove to be a difficult task for a lot of the local nationals. Myself, the terp, and SGT. F took the boy out to the gate where an ambulance was be waiting for us. After a security checkpoint, we went outside the wire and met with the ambulance. I helped put the boy's body into a wooden box, then they loaded him up into the back of the Afghan ambulance and left. The ride back to the hospital was a silent one.

Afghanistan would be the turning point for me in my military career. The irony is that it fell at the tail end of it. Afghanistan was the seventh year of my eight-year military career. I'm not sure if that's a good thing or a bad thing, but that's the way it ended up being. After Afghanistan, I did a MEDRETE in El Salvador, my second tour down there. After that, it was back to work and school. Yet, I'm starting to understand why it took so long for me to see the impacts of war. I think I was too distracted and too busy to notice or realize I had issues after Afghanistan. It was non-stop for me and I never took to the time to unwind. Turns out, I'm not the only one that went through this. The doc at the VA hospital said that we are all born with about 15% likelihood to have depression. That percentage increases about another 50% if a parent was ever diagnosed with depression, and that percentage increases even more if you ever experience a traumatic event in your life, like war. So, if you went to war and didn't come back fucked up, that would be very concerning.

In May of 2016, I was diagnosed with PTSD. Welcome to the club.

Transition to Civilian Life

How many years has it been since you swore an oath to defend the United States of America? It was so long ago that the memory may have become hazy and unfamiliar, like a dream. Bits and pieces may stand out at you and you likely can't recall all of it, but perhaps a few important details. You were in a small room with other young men and women, someone at the front leading the oath. I bet you can't remember if the leader of this group was wearing a uniform or not. Like you, as I spoke the oath, I had two very strong feelings fall over me. One was a sense of duty and pride that I would be taking on such a huge responsibility. My chest swelled, eyes sharp, back straight, and right hand raised. I was taking on a new direction in life and it was going to be great! The other feeling was—I had no fucking idea what I was doing there.

Fast forward eight years later. I'm tired now. I'm not the same highly motivated 18 year old I once was. I'm jaded. I've been dicked over too many times to count. I've been skipped over for promotions but still given extra instructor and duty assignments because I'm too good at my job. I'm also the guy with the most recent combat experience in my section, so I should be the one to give a Power Point presentation for the new kids. I don't care like I used to. Command wants something done? I'll get to it whenever the fuck I feel like it, I'm just here for my soldiers and my check. The same sons of bitches that want to give me orders are the same ones that have been dodging deployments their entire military careers. I'll be the first to admit, I did not want to go to war. I had no passion for combat nor did I want to do my job in the shit storm of Afghanistan. Why would I? I was the same 18 year old kid rolling soldiers on stretchers from the bus to the ICU of Landstuhl Regional Medical Center (LRMC). I saw what war was like, all the troops getting MEDEVAC'd from Fallujah by the plane and busload. Soldiers afraid, in pain, fuming mad because they left their buddies back on the field of war while they got patched up. There have been numerous times where I have had to use my weight to hold a warrior down because the last thing they remember is an explosion going off and now they're in the coldness of Germany being pushed into a hospital, while my skinny ass tries to hold them down and reassure them that they're going to be okay.

No, I didn't want to go to war, and all the Rambo wannabees in my unit that said they wanted to go to war were the first ones to bitch out when their number was called. Some pulled the medical card while others used their continuing education as another deterrent. These were the ones that pissed me off the most, the people who talked all this big game to go down range but didn't have the follow through to go when their name was called. When these same soldiers said they couldn't go, guess who had to take their place? Fuck those guys. I didn't want to go war but it was in my god damn job description, so I went. End rant.

Now it was time to decide if I wanted to continue my glorious career of let downs and ass fucking. It was a tough call to make. I mean, I could give up this great life of never knowing where I would be in a year, constantly losing friends and relationships, being told by family and loved ones that I'm changing, never really being able to finish school and not being able to accomplish my own life goals or become one of "them" — a civilian.

A scene from the movie *Half Baked* comes to mind, where Julio, the patty flipper, of a burger restaurant has had enough of his bullshit job and co-workers: "Fuck you, fuck you, fuck you... you cool, and fuck you, I'm out"!

I ETS'd on October 9, 2010, and if you're a veteran, I'd bet good money you just thought of your own ETS date. I was getting out of the military and planned to never look back. I was going to be my own man and decide my own future. No more Power Point presentations, no more bullshit details, no more incompetent command, no more "we lost your packet" excuses, and no more green weenies! I was done with it all and there was nothing the military could ever do to hurt me again. I would sleep soundly at night for I had the protection of the almighty DD-214 that would keep those wretched military goons at bay. I was free.

Now what the hell would I do?

To be honest, transitioning was scary for me. As excited as I was to break the Army chains from my wrists, I was afraid I was too far removed from the civilian lifestyle to really acclimate to my surroundings. I mean, it's not like you stop thinking like a soldier overnight (I'm not sure that you ever do), but anyone who has served in the military definitely has a different thought process than the majority of civilians. It's not bad or good, better or worse, just different. I think the hardest part about the transition was that for a good while, everything was in black or white and it took me a while to relearn how to think critically. Going back to school would greatly help, but I soon realized how deathly afraid of school I was.

I started at community college and was always anxious before and during class. I think I had a literal fear of going to class. My girlfriend at the time joked that I was worried about a drive-by quizzes. Was that the reason I was always hyper vigilant and had my head on a swivel 24/7? I also had a hard time relating to my younger classmates. At the ripe old age of 25, I had a tendency to be the eldest of my classmates with a lot more life experience. It helped in some social aspects—I made a few friends, dated a few girls but still didn't really let anyone in. I'm a jokester by nature and a social butterfly but realize now that all that time in school, I was going through PTSD, I just didn't know it.

There are times when you can't see what's going on at the moment but years later you can reflect on your actions and decisions, and it hits you like a ton of bricks. I had some serious issues that I never addressed. I had a laundry list of issues and never once considered I wasn't okay. I mean, I came home with all my fingers and toes, I was fine, right?

Life has a way of telling us that things aren't okay. It gives us lots of red flags but I either we are too blinded by love and delusion or we just choose to ignore the signs and continue on the same broken path. For me, and I'm sure a lot of other vets, it all started at the bottom of the bottle.

One thing about us military folk is that we work hard and we play even harder. We love a good drunken night, the more the merrier. Now, I'm sure you've heard of the drunken sailors or the belligerent Marines; alcohol and the military go together like biscuits and gravy. However, what you may not know is how those old drinking habits can get worse once we leave the service. If you're like me, when you got out of the service you had this urge to catch up on life and everything you missed out on. All the parties you missed, all the bar hopping, the sporting events, the hangouts, weddings, birthdays, and deaths. You missed out on a lot since you were away, and now, every day was a chance to party and consume ungodly amounts of alcohol.

All my years of training and preparation had given me the ability to drink all my friends under the table. My mug was never empty, my eyes were never glossy, and there was always time for another round. In the midst of all my partying and drinking, a sudden dependency began to emerge. Things weren't really fun without a cold beer in my hand. I drank and drove—a lot—until it finally caught up with me. Getting a DUI really hurt, not only financially, but I was extremely embarrassed. Even though I was living on my own I had to tell my family. My parents were happy I was okay but I could tell they were shocked and disappointed. I also felt like I had really let my younger siblings down. I'm the eldest and I'm supposed to lead by example. I pleaded with them to learn from my mistakes and make better choices.

After I got my DUI, I had to complete a course and attend Alcoholics Anonymous. I learned a few things there that really stuck with me. The first I learned was that I wasn't alone. All sorts of people from all walks of life get DUIs—professionals, gangsters, cholos, veterans, housewives, underaged drinkers, the wealthy, and the economically disenfranchised. You hear their stories, you share yours, and you all look in awe at the ones with more than eight DUIs (they exist). One of my instructors had 11 DUIs, granted, the majority of these were in the 70s, where a DUI was a small infraction and you only had to pay a small fine. Oh, and my instructor was an army veteran. I'm sure a few of the veterans in your life have had a DUI or two. Are you starting to see a pattern?

Another lesson I learned was that just because you got a DUI doesn't mean you are an alcoholic. However, it does mean that you have alcoholic tendencies. Meaning, you act like an alcoholic when you are careless, and you don't take the appropriate actions to ensure you don't drink and drive. Also, you drink for the wrong reasons, like anger or sorrow— these are sings of alcoholic tendencies as well. DUIs suck all around, but at least you know you aren't the only one, and don't ever think it can't happen to you. Just think about all the times you drove drunk, all the times you made it home in one piece, all the times you woke up and couldn't remember how you got home so you ran outside to inspect your car for damages or blood splatter. So here's my public service announcement: Don't drink and drive. It's not worth it. Calling an Uber, Lyft, or cab is much cheaper than a DUI, trust me on this.

Alcohol is a quick fix on a broken heart and weathered soul. It keeps the sorrow at bay and lets the laughter run freely. I realize now that I drank a lot so that I could laugh and smile again. Nobody likes to be down in the dumps and it's hard to feel sad when you're drinking with your buddies, but alcohol isn't the only quick fix. We all find our temporary Band-Aids we place over our gushing wounds. Booze was one such Band-Aid for me; women were another.

For years I was, "emotionally unavailable." Let's be honest, I was too afraid to commit to a relationship and just wanted to get laid. I also wanted the girlfriend experience without the title or obligations because somehow that felt like it made it easier for me. I think we are all looking for some kind of love to fill our lives with but we rarely are honest with ourselves to admit it. Unfortunately, I used women and sex to fill an empty void in me, as if I was trying to fuck the pain away. And it helped to some degree, meeting different women, having amazing sex, feeling like the sex god that I was; I was kind of like Eros, the god of love, primeval and chaotic. I beckoned women to my bedroom and would please them beyond comprehension. I made sure they were satisfied and left without energy. I always I made a game out of sex, how many times could I make her cum before I did. Looking back now, I think I did that to be wanted, to be lusted after. Nothing feels better that to be wanted, but I wanted more than sex, I just couldn't put my finger on it.

I'd always use the same direct and honest line to get women in bed with me: "I don't have to lie to get what I want. If you want to date and have some fun, I'm your guy, but if you want a boyfriend, you need to look somewhere else." It worked more than you might think. Why did it work? The simple reason was because I wasn't blowing smoke up their ass. I figured, we're all adults here, let's be open and honest so there's less of a chance that anyone's feelings would get hurt... but we all know that rarely works out. I'd tell myself that I didn't want anything serious when I really did. Women would say they were there just for a good time but would get emotionally involved. It happens, we're only human. We can be very complicated creatures exhibiting a wide variety of emotions. For veterans, one of the most common and readily available emotions is anger.

As I said before, I think of myself as a pretty likeable guy; I love to joke and laugh and enjoy a good story. I remember being very patient growing, and for the most part, I still am. However, looking back, I realize there was always one sure way to ignite a very short fuse: be rude to me. It sounds petty and insignificant, I know, but you want to talk about getting "triggered"? Boy oh boy do I have some stories for you.

Now, I like to think I have pretty thick skin. I can take a joke when my buddies start razzing me, that's fine and dandy because it's all said in good fun. Yet, when someone doesn't know me and is rude, disrespectful, or just plain mean to me, I lose my shit. I take this to extremes; it 's as if you just slapped my mother and spit in my father's face. I've gone from calm to murderous intent in 1.5 seconds.

While I was attending community college, I made friends with a young lady who I met in my business calculus class. This gal was a brain. I found out later on that she was attending her last year of high school while attending her last year at community college. She would be graduating high school and obtaining her associates at the same time. I didn't know how she had the mental capacity to do so much at once, but like I said, she was a brain. Needless to say, she was a great study partner. One day we were hanging out in the library of our school, it might have been around finals time. I remember all the students scattered around, shoving their faces in books, cramming away before their next exam. We were chatting, quietly (I know, we shouldn't be talking in the library to begin with) when we heard a loud screech. We looked around, confused, trying to figure out what we had heard or what had just happened. We went back to our quiet conversation when a minute later a young college student stood up, turned around, and shouted at the top of his lungs, "You guys need to shut the fuck up, people are trying to study here." I guess this kid had shushed us earlier and we didn't recognize it. Now, it took me a second to process what was going on, all the while I had slowly stood up and was staring him down. My friend was not as calm, sitting there a deer in the headlights look, barely able to utter that she was sorry. Now I was pissed. This guy had made my sweet and innocent friend, the least confrontational person in the world, so afraid that she couldn't stop shaking. "And yelling at us is going to bring the noise level down?" I said. I stood my ground, ready for a fight in a library full of students looking up from their textbooks to watch the event unfold. Do I smell popcorn?

"Well you guys just need to shut the fuck up," he snarled at us. I wasn't happy. So in all of my vast amounts of wisdom and training of de-escalation tactics, I said, "Why don't you come over here and shut me up?" The students looked like kittens watching a laser pointer moving from left to right as the tough guy and myself exchanged words. Now they stared at him, waiting for his rebuttal. "Naw, man, I can't get into trouble. I can't get into a fight." Now the kittens all stared at me. "Then shut the fuck up and sit back down," I firmly told him. The eyes were on him, yet again. "Well you guys need to just shut the fuck—" I cut him off before he completed his last statement: "Like I said, you can come over here and shut me up, if not, sit your bitch ass down." A student in the distance say, "Damn." He sat down and went about his business. The whole time I was having this exchange, my friend had been pulling at my arm hoping that I would change my mind. However, if you're like me, you know you can't switch back. You have to see it through to the end.

Looking back now, I was in the wrong and it was a stupid situation to get involved in. The kid was probably stressed and wanted to do his best on his finals like everybody else in the library. In his immaturity, instead of asking politely for us quiet down or take the conversation outside, he let his frustration get the better of him, which ended up getting the better of me too. Imagine if I had gotten into a fight with the kid? Sure, let's say I whooped his ass, whooped his ass so hard that anytime he saw me he'd piss himself. That would have brought on a whole slew of problems for me—getting kicked out of school, arrested, possibly losing benefits, and so on.

Another time that was totally not my fault, I was simply trying to find a parking spot at a local grocery store. As I was driving, I saw a couple pushing a stroller. They were passing me by and pulled a little closer to the stalls as to give them more room to walk by. I gently passed them, and as I did, I heard the man yell, "Watch where you're going pendejo!" Danger! Danger! Danger! Combat mode, activate! I slammed on the breaks, felt my blood go nuclear, my muscles tense, and my eyes lock on. I put my car in park, stepped out, turned to the asshole who would dare disrespect me, and yelled, "What the fuck did you say?" The guy seemed stunned that I reacted the way I did. He turned around with a flustered look, turned back, and continued walking. As this happened, I realized just who I was yelling at. This guy must have been at least 6'2", easily weighed 280-300 lbs, and looked like an upright polar bear. Mind you, I'm only 5'8" and 165 lbs on a good day. Yet, at the moment, his height, weight, and the sheer size of the man didn't register. I knew if it came down to it, I'd leave him in a bloody puddle as he desperately tried to grasp for air. Call it anger, call it arrogance, but that's what I thought in the moment. The guy kept walking with his lady and kid. I yelled a few more profanities in his direction, hoping he would turn around. He didn't, thank God.

Who knows how that would have played out. As tough as I thought I was, this guy could have snapped me like a twig. Maybe he was one hell of a fighter, maybe I would make a mistake during the fight and let my guard down and miss the wicked haymaker coming down on me. What if he had a gun? What if I had won the fight and his lady pressed charges and I was arrested? Was all this uncertainty worth my pride and hurt feelings? After the family continued walking, I got back in my car, drove to a parking spot, and yelled my lungs out. I felt so stupid, immature, and weak. I let someone's words take complete control of me and I hated myself for it. I was still mad at the guy, not because he hurled an insult at me, but because I thought to myself, what if I had a gun? What if I was some gang banger who didn't care and killed him and his family because I felt disrespected? There are too many variables when it comes to confrontation and uncontrolled anger. It won't end well for anyone. So my advice for you is: Don't lose control of the situation, and don't give anyone the power to manipulate you and dictate your next action. I'm sure you've heard people say, "They made me do it!" Bullshit. We are all responsible for our own actions. Be mindful of your environment and the people around you, and for God's sakes, just be a nice person. It doesn't cost you anything to be nice, but it could cost you everything to be an asshole.

Another symptom of being an asshole is that it can increase your chances of having substantially less funds in your bank account. You really think anyone wants to work with a jerk like you? Let's be real now, dumbass Billy over in receivables has a better chance of keeping his job and getting a raise not because he's good at his job but because people actually like the guy. You may not like him because he's so goddamn nice and positive that flowers grow behind his every step, rainbows shoot out of his ass, and he won't stop talking about his hippie yoga that Janet is obviously way more into than your crass war stories. Billy will still have a job, might even bang Janet if he tones down the hippie shit, and you'll be assed out of a job with no money except maybe the disability check you receive, all because you won't change your fucking attitude.

Being out of the military and broke off your ass really sucks. Living on your dad's couch and waiting for that measly weekend reserve check because you can't find a job sucks even more. As much as the military has trained us to have contingency plans, we tend to forget that when we go full civilian (you never go full civilian). I think it goes back to us just trying to "catch up" on life so much that we lose sight of planning for our future. Remember, there is no sergeant to tell you what you'll be doing for the next year. You need to figure that shit out on your own, or at the very least, learn how to ask for help. Put away the anger and open your ears, you might learn a thing or two.

Unfortunately, anger is what defines a lot of us vets, but in my opinion, it's a mask, a shield if you will, to hide our true feelings of pain and sorrow. As soldiers, marines, seaman, airman, and yes, even the coast guardsmen, we are trained to be mentally and physically tough. We are trained to go to war, to kill, and to not hesitate when we squeeze the trigger. In our indoctrination into the military, we set aside our emotions of guilt, pain, sorrow, remorse, pity, and empathy. We focus on building our strength, we focus on killing, we focus on our willingness to die for the person to our left and our right, and in doing so, we suppress all non-essential feelings and emotions. We go to war, experience horrifying ordeals while we eliminate the enemy, while we try to stop our best friend from bleeding out, while we read a letter from our sweetheart that says "It's just not working out," and even while realizing that we won't be home for the holidays. We have wave after wave after wave of emotional crashes that we have to ignore because we need to be vigilant and have our weapon at the ready. We have been reprogrammed and set on overdrive for the full duration of war so that when we finally get to go home and hang up the uniform, we're expected to smoothly transition back into society. In reality, it's more like going 100 mph and realizing that somebody cut the brake lines, and there's a brick wall coming up fast with your name on it.

Maybe this is why we drink so much. The only time we can let our guard down long enough to feel something other than pain and anger is found at the bottom of a bottle. We let our emotions out in the most untherapeutic ways and end up sealing ourselves right back up; we pick up where we left off every time we take another swig of that whiskey or beer.

All the pain and sorrow is too much to process and too scary to acknowledge. Maybe we did something we're ashamed of. Maybe we have seen something we can't un-see. Perhaps there is an inner struggle that rages and we don't know how to deal with it, so instead, we drink to forget.

Why We Cling to the Angry Veteran

For a lot of us, myself included, when we meet our angry veteran, we take refuge within the persona we have developed. It becomes very appealing actually because nobody wants to mess with a vet who looks like a vet. You know the kind—those who have that cold blank stare because the twinkle has burned out; the lines of age and exhaustion are more prominent upon their faces; their posture is tall and upright, still able react at a moment's notice; facial hair is thick and coarse; wearing a dirty old camo ball cap, blacked out sunglasses, and a military motto t-shirt. This has become our new uniform, our coat of armor. This tells the world to stay 100 meters back or you will be shot! This tells the world, "I still got it, I'm still tough, I'm protected, I'm still apart of something greater than myself."

I believe that for the majority of humans, we need to feel a sense of belonging. We need to have an association to a group of people, to feel that we belong to something bigger than ourselves. In the military, we are constantly reminded of the need to belong. We are taught that there is nothing greater in the world than being a member of those that serve their country. Not everyone has what it takes to do what we do, and for that, we have joined a brotherhood unlike any other. I loved being a member of the U.S. Army. There was pride in my eyes when I would tell people I was a soldier, the places I had been, and the work that I had done. You could be in a room full of doctors, lawyers, business owners, and politicians, but when you announce that you are in the military, everyone is intrigued and thinks the world of you. Normally, this comes from those who have never served. They look in awe because perhaps they wanted to join at one point. You hear all the time, " I was going to join but..." For whatever reason, these people never joined, and for that, envy the uniform and those belonging to the core. So yeah, I was very proud.

You know when it was I felt the best? When I felt on top of the world to be able to call myself a U.S. soldier? When I was around kids. When kids saw me in uniform, they didn't see a soldier, they saw a superhero. Their eyes would widen, their mouths hanging open as they'd slowly approach me to ask, "Are you in the army?" The sun would shine off of my perfectly polished teeth as I'd smile down upon them. You could hear "The Star-Spangled Banner" begin to play as an American flag waved behind me, chest out, fists resting on my hips, eyes to the sky as I rested one boot on Plymouth rock. I would kneel to their level, look them straight in the eyes and say in my most heroic voice, "I sure am." Their response was always the same: "Wooooowww." They saw me as a superhero, and I played the role to a T. I always carried some stickers or patches for just such an occasion. I'd let them wear my hat and explain what the patches and insignias on my uniform meant. The mothers would be very grateful and happy to see their children so excited. They'd always ask if I wouldn't mind posing for a picture with their children. This was my favorite parts of the job. I felt taller, stronger, and like I was a better person. Can you imagine? These random kids made my childhood fantasy of becoming a superhero into a reality. I want that back but I can't have it anymore. It came with the uniform and I can no longer wear the uniform. I'm not a soldier, I'm not in the army anymore, and I can no longer be a part of the military. My time is done and I have to hang up the uniform, along with the cape. I no longer belong. However, I do belong to another group now.

The best of the worst. The silent heroes of wars forgotten. The broken and tired. The angry drunken bastards who feel more comfortable in dive bar than a five-star restaurant. The ones who still like to get their hands dirty and, for some stupid reason, do things the hard way. I belong to you and you to me. We are our own brotherhood now, a band of veterans, and I love you disgruntled sons of bitches.

From one family to another, us veterans find refuge in each other because we understand one another. We worked for different branches, wore different uniforms, had different jobs, but we were all in the shit at one point in time. We have earned each other's respect and admiration. It's a different community, a warm and loving community where you curse and insult one another face to face but behind your backs give applause and admiration. We are all just as lost and in pain as the next and will accept you whether you progress in life or not. A broken home for a broken few, and nothing feels more welcoming to know that all these people have lost just as much as you. They get it.

It's great to know that we have this community; it helps us out in so many ways. For one, we get to belong again. We're not in the military anymore, but we still act like it at times. We still call each other by our last names and sometimes by rank. We still use that military lingo, hell, we still call each other "Blue Falcons." We still like to shoot our guns and we still like to complain about the military, even if we've been out for years. All of this is great and it can be seen as a transitional crutch for those exiting the military and into the civilian life. You won't be alone, but the downside is that you may be relying on this persona too much and for too long.

I get it. It's scary to let go. As much as we grab our junk and give the middle finger to the military and say we're never going back, we miss it. We miss our brothers and sisters. We miss the adventure and the traveling. I miss the paid traveling (well, maybe not Afghanistan so much). I don't know of many jobs, that don't require degrees or years of experience, that will pay you to travel. God, I wish someone would pay me to go to Japan. I'm still waiting to go. Maybe you're like me and miss wearing the uniform, not because it's the most fashionable thing around but because I didn't have to think about how to dress myself. These days I still ask my wife if something looks good on me. It was so much easier to just throw on the uniform and head to work. Try working for a place that doesn't have a uniform policy and see how difficult it is to dress yourself in the morning after eight years of wearing the same old uniform.

I remember when I first started working for a local school district as in instructional assistant. I was predominantly working with special needs children that had physical limitations but were cognitively at the same level as general education students. My first day to work I showed up in a full suit and tie. I wasn't given any real guidance as to how to appear so I figured I should play it safe and look my best. Fresh cut, shaven, aviators, and a suit to match; I looked pretty damn good cleaned up. As I walked across the campus to my duty station I noticed many of the staff kept staring at me with puzzled and worried expressions. Later that day, I heard there were rumors going around that I was from the district office doing an audit. Others thought I was a new principal. A few kids thought I was a cop and were very careful around me. One little boy came up to me and after a minute of inspecting my appearance sheepishly uttered the words, "Are you like, a secret agent or something?" I lowered myself to his ear and whispered, "If I tell you, I'd have to kill you." I wish I could have seen the look on this kid's face but I had to keep on walking to pull off my little joke.

Like all things, we have to learn to adapt to change and let's keep it real—the military is constantly changing. Think about all the command decisions that change just to show up to formation. Your platoon will end up at formation two hours in advance because people are always trying to get there early. We're constantly changing our uniform so that some general can get a bullet point on their annual review. Remember "hurry up and wait"? How many times did you have to leave the tarmac because it wasn't good weather for killing? Looking back now, we were pretty good at dealing with change.

You can take the soldier out of the military but you can't take the military out of the soldier. It's cheesy, I know, but if you think about leaving the military in this context you won't have to be fearful of losing the military. The military will always have a special place in your heart, whether you want it or not. You've gone through too much to not let it be a part of you. However, it is only a part of you, it's not what defines you. You are much more than just a jarhead or a war dog. So as you hang with your veteran buddies and keep in touch with old comrades that still serve, don't be afraid to let go a little bit. Find out who you are or who you can become. If you don't, you won't survive.

Sometimes, the fear of leaving the military can be so overwhelming that holding onto the angry veteran is a safer default. Yet, many veterans choose to not acclimate to civilian society. Why? I think it's because some veterans don't want to accept that they are now a civilian again. It takes some getting used to, but there are a lot of perks to being civilian again. No top brass telling you what to wear and where to be all the time, no more weapon cleaning, no more guard duty, no more B-rations or MREs. Carpet! Oh, how I was so happy to have carpet under my bare feet again. A restroom in my room, sweet baby Jesus! No more having to walk a block in the pitch black darkness of Afghanistan to use the restroom. I'm telling you, figuring out how to do our taxes and apply for jobs might be a pain in the ass at first but all the other perks are totally worth it.

You can get used to becoming a civilian again, it's just like riding a bicycle—you'll shake a bit at first but you'll be cruising in no time.

One area that I've personally run into that made it difficult for me to let go of the angry veteran is that I lacked direction. I also lacked the self-dependence that I once had (very little mind you) because I relied on the military for far too long. If you think about it, I was 17 and a half when I joined; I got out of the military at 26. For most of my adult life, I was told what to do, all the time. From my parents to my superiors. I always had someone to give me their opinion, even when it was unwarranted. This made it harder to be more independent. Even now, I feel that I've really just begun developing my critical thinking skills for my own life decisions. It's much easier to have someone manage your life, but if you really want to grow and evolve, you need to learn to truly think for yourself, even if that means that your ideas may differ from that of your fellow veterans.

I believe that the angry veteran is a transitional stage that we have created due to fear and pain. We don't want to lose our past but are too afraid to tackle the future. This gives us a bit of a buffer so that we can transition as best as we can into society again. However, the problems really come about to those who are afraid to transition or refuse to. You will always be a part of your past, it will always live inside of you, but you are the one that controls that aspect of yourself, you are the one in charge. Don't let the anger and pain determine your future. It's okay to accept your new life, you can always look back to the past and look at the good times. Accept the bad times as a part of your time on this world and embrace the fond memories that you made. Holding onto all that negativity will only beget more negativity. So, try to relax a bit, share a smile, and have a beer, or do what I like to do—go for a walk and clear your mind. Life is a lot more beautiful if you're willing to look at all the beauty in this world.

Battle Buddy in Need

We all have moments of desperation and anguish, times where we wish we had someone close by, not necessarily to fix a problem but just to be there to hear us out or simply let us know we are not alone. If you're like me, sometimes pride can hold you back from reaching out to someone. We even reject the hand offered to us by our most cherished of relationships. Why, you may ask? We don't want to burden anyone with our problems. We know you have a lot going on as it is. We know that you're trying to make ends meet, studying for your degree, working odd hours to put food on the table, going through a divorce, planning a wedding, dealing with your own health; you have way too much to deal with and my little problem isn't that important. It's no big deal. I'll be fine. But it is a big deal. It could be the difference between life and death. It could be the difference between a life filled with happiness, friends, and family, or alone full of anger with nothing but a bottle in your hand.

However, I'm willing to bet that if the tables were turned and you knew someone who needed a place to stay, words of encouragement, or a beer and some good hearing ears, there is nothing in this world that would stop you from being there for them. So why can't they be there for you? Ditch the pride and realize you are worthy of being helped. You are just as human as the next, and at times, you just need someone to talk to. They won't fix you overnight, but you will begin to heal and it will feel good to get some things off your chest. Little by little, you start to open up again and the simple pleasures of life seem a bit more spectacular. We all need help, and as much as you need to help those around you, don't forget to ask for help when you need it.

I'm glad I had the opportunity to help fellow veterans when I had the chance. I didn't do anything heroic, I didn't shower them with booze and tits; I listened. I was just there when they called or sent me a text. I send a random dick picture of some burley man just for shits and giggles. It was my way of saying, "Hey buddy, how are you? I hope you liked the dick." We'd have a great laugh and catch up a bit on life. It wasn't always positive news but it kept a conversation going and I knew they were okay, for the time being at least. However, there are times where I feel so glad that I didn't ignore a call… one time in particular.

I received a call from a buddy of mine who had done a tour in Iraq. We joined the military at different times but had a long history. He was, drunk, scared, and feeling helpless. He had just gotten an offer for a government job and was now holding a gun to his head. Confusing, I know. I asked why was he so upset, telling him that it sounded like good news to me and how he was better off putting the gun down. The thing is, my buddy smokes weed to sleep. He says it's the only thing that keeps the nightmares at bay. He's done somethings he's not proud of and they come back to haunt him at night. Drinking doesn't help him—I've seen him drunk, it's not pretty. You have a friend like that too, don't you? The one where you should have cut off five beers and two shots ago. The kind of person that the more they drink, the more the demons take over their body and they starts saying and doing some shit that you just hang your head in disbelief. You know them very well. Maybe it's you. My buddy was crying at this point and still trying to comprehend whether pulling the trigger would really solve all his problems, or at the very least let him sleep peacefully. He was angry, sad, at the end of his rope, and in need of someone to listen to him. He could have called any number of other vets but he called me, and I answered. I would hear him out for as long as he needed. Thankfully this friend is still alive today, but we all know too well the ones that fell through the cracks, the ones that were not reached in time. Be sure to check in on each other. You could be saving someone's life, or your own.

There are times where we need to be there for our buddies, perhaps not as great a need as a life or death situation but still a need deserving of our immediate attention. I've ran into a few instances where a buddy of mine would have what I called "angry tantrums," Sometimes they boil over with range and anger. Hate and the thought of ripping someone's skin from their flesh filled their eyes. All they saw was red. I bet you know this kind of person too.

I knew a guy like this, an army dog like me. We met at local car meets. Great guy, super nice and easy going; you never would have though he had gone to war, but then his anger would surface. It would happen randomly, out of the blue, for no apparent reason. We'd all be hanging out a local car meet, and from the corner of my eye I would see him stomp off, shaking his fists and gritting his teeth as if he was trying to contain a nuclear explosion going off on inside of him. He was desperate to contain it but his outbursts and look of sheer anguish was drawing attention. One time when it happened, I walked up to him and tried to figure out what was going on. He simply replied that sometimes he gets really angry. Perhaps someone said or did something he didn't like, maybe he scuffed his new white Jordans or maybe he was reminded of the war that left him defeated and unsettled. To this day I can't remember what it was about. It could have been nothing at all that set him off but he was going through it and I wasn't sure what to do. I had no clear cut answer on how to calm him down or how to still the raging bull within him, so I talked about me. I talked to him about my anger, my dissatisfaction with the military and what I had experienced in Afghanistan. I noticed as I was telling him all of this, he continued to pace back and forth but his eyes were now locked on me. Yet, they were different than before. They weren't full of anger or hungry for a fight, they seemed almost sad. His body was still angry, but I think I was reaching his heart. By telling my stories of pain and anguish, my suffrage, the focus was now on me and less on his own battles. I could tell he felt sorry for me, and maybe he realized he wasn't alone in all this misery. He stopped pacing, stopped shaking, and became still and quiet, intently listening to what I had to say. The spell had been broken and I was even able to get a few laughs out of him. Is this a cure-all for angry tantrums? Probably not, but I believe that it is a good start. I took the focus off of his own anger by sharing my issues. The point is to talk it out. You don't have to be the best public speaker or the have the most eloquent words, just being there and listening does wonders for someone in need.

We all have our inner explosions—some can be loud and obvious, others as subtle as a butterfly landing or silent as the moon. We've already discussed my loud and angry moments, but there were my days where I woke up, wanting to go to war. No reason really, but perhaps it was easier to deal with war than people some days.

Other times, my rage would build in my sleep and in my dreams. Sometimes I'd dream of war, sometimes of death. I'd dream of killing the enemy or holding dead children in my arms as I cried in pain. It was never much that I could remember but a few fleeting details. I could smell the blood, feel the heat from the Afghan sun, taste the salty sweat as it ran down my helmet's chin strap. I'd wake up in the middle of the night, yelling or crying, covered in sweat, cold and shaky. At times I might remember what I dreamt, while other times I only remembered the pain from the dream. It was always hard to go back to sleep after a dream like that. Once while I was still in Afghanistan, back when I still had a gal back home waiting for me, I was in my hooch on my little hard wood bed, and I must have been dreaming but it felt so real. I could smell my girlfriend, her scent of a lightly sweetened flower with a mix of lotion. She was lying next to me, I could feel her body heat and butt pressing against my back. I rolled over to hug her, to tell her how much I had missed her and I grabbed nothing but the blanket. I jumped up and looked for her in the sheets, I was lost and confused. Nothing was familiar to me, I didn't know where I was or how I had gotten in this little room. I started to panic and in a matter of seconds it all came back to me. "Fuck! I'm still here." It was the worst feeling in the world, to think you had someone you held so dear at arm's reach, just to have them snatched away from you before you could lay a finger on them. It felt like having your hair yanked out and dangled in front of you.

It's a horrible feeling to have these kinds of nightmares. They were always painful and made it harder and harder to go to sleep. It was even worse when I would hurt other people in my sleep. Once I was seeing this gal, it was casual but I enjoyed the company as I slept at night. I think I needed someone there at night. One morning, she told me that I had choked her in the middle of the night. I tend to twitch and almost convulse when I sleep and must have had my arm around her. She said I fiercely grabbed her by the neck and pulled back. What she was describing was a rear naked choke hold. Poor thing was scared out of her mind as I tried to snuff the life out of her. Luckily, she said, it only lasted a second or two before I fell back to sleep. I felt like a piece of shit. In my opinion it's never alright for a man to put his hands on a lady. Call me chauvinistic or old school but that's how I feel about that. I kept apologizing over and over again. She wasn't mad at me, she didn't blame me for what happened. She knew of my military background, so to some degree she understood. We didn't see each other much after that. I don't blame her.

Another time, a different gal I was dating was coming over to my place after work. I left the door unlocked for her to let herself in. I must have been exhausted because I fell asleep waiting for her. I'm naturally a very light sleeper. However, I didn't hear her climb that obnoxiously loud stair case, open the screen door, open the door, close both doors, or open my bedroom door. I woke up when I felt her gently sit down next to me. I sprang up, cocked my fist back and lunged forward with all my might. I was inches away from her face when I realized it was her. I came to. Her normally green eyes had turned icy blue as a single tear streamed down her face. I fell back on the bed and passed out. I woke up a second later and she was there, crying, trying to figure out what had just happened. It all came back to me and I realized what I had almost done. She was sobbing and I was holding her as I tried to console her, all the while I kept thinking I was the biggest piece of shit that ever walked the Earth. I later found out that she wasn't really crying because of me, but because she had previously been in an abusive relationship and this incident had given her flashbacks from the beatings she had received.

We didn't last much longer either, not because I almost rearranged her nose, but because I wasn't able to open up to someone who wanted nothing more than to love me for all eternity. It took me a while to get over the loss of her. I kept kicking myself in the ass for not being able to love. She was great, and had it all, but it wasn't meant to be. A few years ago, I found out she was happily married, and to be honest, it made me smile. I was really happy for her. If she would have stuck around with me, she may have never met her husband. I hope they have a long and happy marriage.

Moral of the story, kids, check in on each other. We all go through things differently. We all express pain in different manners and have different degrees of pain. Be sure to always check in on your buddies, check in on their families, and for Pete's sake, let people in. It's a two-way street and it only works if you allow others to check in on you and see how you are doing. Otherwise you come off as the prick-know-it-all. I know I've been that guy before. I try to listen more these days. Try to do the same.

They Won't Understand

Well, no shit. How do you expect anyone to truly understand what we veterans have been through? How do you expect anyone who hasn't worn the uniform, held their salutes for the fallen, or sacrificed everything for their country? How do you truly expect "them" to understand the pain, agony, pride, courage, fear, and exhaustion that comes with swearing an oath to your country and a willingness to give your life for it. Bottom line is, you can't expect them to understand nor should you expect them to understand what we veterans go through. They will never truly understand, I'm here to tell you, that's okay. What matters is that they try to understand. They want to understand, they want to hear us out and be there for us. They're not going to "fix" us, nor are they going to make all the pain go away but they provide us an emotional outlet for us to relinquish all the bottled up pain and sorrow we have inside. The sooner you pull your head out of your ass and realize that people all around you just want to be there for you, the sooner you can start on your path to living a happier and healthier life. So unfuck yourself (insert knife hand here), swallow your pride, and open your ears and mind to someone other than the same broken vet you get drunk with.

It takes a lot to go through war. It takes even more to work out the emotional devastation we go through. You can't honestly believe that you can work it out all on your own. Maybe there are some badasses out there that I'm unaware of, but for the rest of us mortals, we could use the help. Sometimes, that helping hand, that open ear, or that warm embrace can come from the most unlikely people.

I was taking leave from Afghanistan, going home for the holidays. I was super lucky and grateful that I would be able to spend time at home with family and friends for the holidays. Not everyone gets that privilege. I had just come off an 18-hour flight from Kuwait and was now in Hartsfield-Jackson Atlanta International Airport. I was tired, dirty, smelly, and I'm sure I had horrendous breath. When you fly from Kuwait on an AC-130 for that long, you're lucky enough if you get to take a piss during flight. You and about few hundred other joes, all squished together like canned sardines with all of your gear and luggage piled on top of you. There is no check-in luggage, no cocktails or nuts, no inflight movie. The closest thing to entertainment is watching a soldier's head bob back and forth as they choke on their own saliva. It's cold, loud, and just plain miserable on those flights, but hey, I was on American soil now and one step closer to being home.

I was in one of those mini stores you see all over airport terminals that sell magazines, snacks, and beverages. I had just bought some gum to cover the halitosis wreaking from my mouth. As I walked outside the shop, I tried to get my bearings straight in order to figure out where my next terminal would be. As I read the displays, searching for my flight back to Orange County, CA, I felt something touch my lower back. I quickly turned around (kind of startled) and saw nothing, but then I looked down. A little girl, no older than 10 years old was in front of me. She had these brilliant ocean blue eyes, long blonde hair, and a porcelain face that held a great big smile. She lunged at me, hugged me tightly and told me, "Thank you for keeping me safe". It hit me like a ton of bricks and my heart sank. As filthy as I was, as tired and unapproachable as I appeared, she saw through all of that and wanted to show me that she cared about me. It took everything in me to not break down in the middle of that airport and cry. I didn't know how desperately I needed that hug. How much that one moment would impact me for the rest of my life. I needed to be held, I needed to be loved, and in that one moment, this little girl knew exactly what I needed to make me feel a little bit better. After she ran off with her family, I was left there with my thought and realized: it was all worth it. Everything was worth it, for her. All that I endured, all that I would endure, all that I would lose and gain. All the sacrifice, all of it! It was worth it because of her. I would do it all again because I knew I was helping keep this innocent child safe. I still get emotional reliving that moment. It was one of the most powerful and impactful moments of my life.

Little girl, if you happen to read this. Just know, your hug meant the world to me. You saved me. You gave me hope. You helped me carry on. You helped me release some of that pain I carried with me for so long. I thank you for that, I love you for that and I will always carry a special place for you in my heart.

Guys, maybe we got it all wrong? Maybe people understand more than we think? Pain is pain. Sorrow is sorrow. You don't have to go through war to have empathy for someone else's hardship. A child can recognize when someone is upset or lonely and all they can offer is a hug, but that hug is more powerful than any of us truly understand. Children see pain and want to help and I don't think we really grow out of that. Life isn't perfect and we've all been dealt a shitty hand at different points in our lives. We are left with reminders of that pain, scars that never fade away. Other people carry scars across their bodies too, and maybe they don't understand how you received your scars but they understand scars nonetheless. We carry a heart of stone because we don't want to burden anyone else with it, and we don't share the weight, even with those who have sworn to always be at our sides.

The most important person in our life is our significant other. We make a commitment to that person and they to us, a commitment that we would always be there for one another. For the good and the bad, the fun and the grim. Relationships come with baggage from both sides and they aren't always so obvious to see, let alone understand. Like the corpse flower, some issues take years to blossom, I know mine did. For me, relationships came and went; some ended and were out of my control, while others were a result of my own undoing. Yet, for the ones that were there when I needed to be held, reassured, and listened to, I'm so ever thankful. Now, I am fortunate to have found a soulmate who helps carry the burden of my past and still loves me nonetheless. I always say, "Because of her, I can finally sleep." In my opinion, communicating to your partner about your pain and experiences can actually strengthen a bond. On the same token, not communicating can lead to separation or divorce. I've known a few vets who've lost the love of their life because they could not open up to their spouses. Some have remarried, some are still alone. Yet, do you really want to jeopardize your relationship because you don't think your other half would understand? Is it fair that they were not give the chance to hear you out and to try to help mend your broken soul? Think about all the times where you complained that you "never got to do your job." Don't you think your partner might think the same thing? Don't we all want to do the best that we can in everything that we do? Why wouldn't our partners want the same in our relationships? If there is one thing I learned in the military, it's that you need to let soldiers do the job they were trained for. Relationships can fall into that same mentality. A spouse isn't just there to screw you, feed you, and take care of all the other things you can't or won't do; they are there to be your cornerstone. You should be theirs too.

It's hard to open up to people we are so close to because we're afraid of disappointing them or we fear their judgment. I think the biggest concern of all is the fear of rejection from someone we hold so dear. Well, it's going to happen sooner or later. Let's be honest, none of us are made of sunshine, shitting rainbows as we run butt naked across a field of four-leaf clovers. We are flawed, very, very flawed and if someone can look at you and think, "Yeah, they're pretty fucked up, they got some shitty attributes, a horrendous credit score, and a troubled past, but this bastard is mine," that's love, baby, and if you have someone in your life who can look passed all the mountains of bullshit you've brought along for the ride and still like you enough to screw you, don't fuck it up. Open your goddamn mouth and talk to them. Otherwise, Jody might be sending your boo a friend request.

In the end, I honestly believe we need to be around people that care about us. We do need our time alone, we need our hobbies and need to get our weekly fix of anime, no doubt about that. However, the more we escape into our angry veteran, the more we bury ourselves in isolation. Nobody wants to hang around tough guy Eddie all the time, talking about how kickass he was in the military and how back in his day the military made real dogs of war. Don't be that guy, please. Learn to be more than the angry vet you hide behind, and learn to open up to the ones that really care and are trying to understand. They may never truly understand what you went through or how you feel, and that's okay. They want to show you support and love. That's what family and friends do, and once you start to heal a little bit, once you start to see there is more than the raging anger inside of you, maybe then you can start to show others the light you have seen. We all have layers to who we are, and at times, we need help to pull those layers back to get to know ourselves again. Wouldn't you want to help those in need as well? Don't you want to help the ones on the brink of divorce or suicide? Don't you have buddies going through the same torture that you have been enduring all these years? Aren't they worth trying to help? Aren't they worth trying to help yourself? Well, now it's time for you to lead by example.

Tacti-Cool Joe, the Operator

You know him, you love him, you idolize him, you buy his shitty t-shirts and stickers—introducing for your viewing pleasure and entertainment, Joe, the tacti-cool operator!!!

The crowd of angry veterans applaud and cheer in harmony.

Now, they say imitation is the greatest form of flattery, but these full battle rattle, tactical panty, Oakley wearing, extra magazine carrying wannabe rangers should not be looked to as a source of relevant, veteran bravado. I get it, the gear is shiny and olive drab. That's cool bro. They have nice long beards and wear shmedium t-shirts with skulls and flags that only cost $29.99, plus shipping and handling. Epic dude! They seem to use the same lingo and phrases that we do. They drink beer! I drink beer too! They're like me!? They shoot guns! I shoot guns too! They're like me!? Brah, did we just become best friends!?

To me, a lot of the Tacti-Cool Joe's fancy themselves battle-hardened warriors, all geared up to drink beer and make Facebook/YouTube videos. Some are actually pretty funny, while some give a negative connotation of angry veterans. Granted, there are a lot of us with real issues out there who need help, and that doesn't exactly help our case either. I honestly don't believe that feeding the fire of angry veterans with guys like this helps. It just keeps that overdrive switch on, and many of us might pick up extra bad habits along the way as we follow Tactic-cool Joe and his buddies.

Now, before some of you vets get your panties in a bunch, I'm not knocking veterans for being this way. If you're a vet and this is how you roll, that's you. I still don't think it helps the veteran community, but that's my opinion. Some of you guys are comedians, and it's hilarious, but sometimes the funniest people find themselves in the clown's paradox. What I really disagree with is that some of the Tactic-cool Joes that have never served in the armed forces, but they seem to imply that they have or omit that fact. How? By dressing like us, acting like us, doing veteran things, which, in reality, lots of civilians do. A lot of these same people are the same ones that say, "I was going to join but...(insert excuse)." Again, it's not a bad thing to not have joined the military. Some of us were never meant to join and that's okay. As my wise and dysfunctional cousin would say, "You don't gotta fake it to kick it." What I don't agree with is the almost would-be warriors that seem to ramp up the veteran community in the hopes of selling t-shirts or clicks and likes. As humans, we tend to personify our idols and role models. Just think about your kids if you have any, who do they watch and learn from? Who do they idolize, and do they carry any characteristics from that persona? It's like I've been saying all along in this book—being an angry veteran is only a part of who you are, but it does not define you. So if you keep indulging in these pretend G.I Joes, you'll continue to bury yourself in the only mentality you allow yourself to know.

One thing I've noticed with Tati-Cool Joe and the would-be warriors is that they all have the same guise and attitude. They're tough, hard, manly-men who run their dominions with an iron fist. Their way or the highway, macho men. Yet, it seems like they have to be overly masculine for no apparent reason. They are never seen defending the weak. Never would they dare show themselves talking about their true feelings to friends or loved ones. Instead, they humiliate the very idea that a man can be anything but manly as fuck! To me, that screams fear, that screams self-doubt, a lack of love and positive male role models. Men are more than capable of showing emotions other than brute force and beer-fueled rage. My parents divorced when I was kid so I was lucky enough to have two fathers in my life. My father, who gave me life, who taught me logic, politics, history, patience, and a love for cultures; and my second father, who helped raise me and taught me about auto and motorcycle repair, guns, camping, video games, and how to enjoy life. I was fortunate to have two very different men in my life to teach me how to be a man, two men that made one hell of a dad. Sometimes I would learn through their mistakes, and other times through my own.

Men are a lot more complex than we make ourselves out to be. Do you know how difficult it is to always be tough? To always look hard as shit? God, my chest and shoulders kill me from all that flexing. Damn, that pink glazed donut really looks tasty but I don't want anyone thinking I'm some soy boy for wanting it. Geez, that's gotta be a stressful life, and it kind of makes sense as to why you are so unhappy. You won't even allow yourself the simple pleasure of smelling a flower or playing dolls with your child. Want to show the world how manly you can be? Want to step up to the plate and show what you're really made of? Tell your fellow vet that you love them and will always be there for them. Hug your significant other and thank them for being in your life. Hold your children and reassure them you will always love them, no matter what path in life they take.

Be more than an angry veteran; be a man.

PTSD

Uptodate.com defines Post Traumatic Stress Disorder as: "the complex somatic, cognitive, affective, and behavioral effects of psychological trauma." PTSD is characterized by intrusive thoughts, nightmares and flashbacks of past traumatic events, avoidance of reminders of trauma, hypervigilance, and sleep disturbance, all of which lead to considerable social, occupational, and interpersonal dysfunction."

Reading this hits a few red flags for me. I can look back at my past and realize all the bread crumbs that lead me to the VA hospital in Long Beach to talk with a psychiatrist. It wasn't anything dramatic that got me there. Well, that DUI thing maybe, but that's not the point! The point is what got me thinking I should see someone was that I couldn't sleep. I was very restless, and I had a hard time falling asleep and staying asleep. I would wake up fatigued, sore, and feeling like I only had slept for 20 minutes. It was really strange to me because in the military, I was able to fall asleep anywhere—and I mean ANYWHERE. If you've served, you know what I mean. A 30-minute ride to the range? In 2 minutes, I've fallen asleep on the ammo can I was carrying on my lap. Waiting for training to begin? That patch of rocks and gravel under the Humvee looks pretty comfortable. Transport by cattle truck in basic training? Let me borrow your arm bro, I need a place to lay my head. If falling asleep was an Olympic sport, U.S. service members would be killing the competition.

Alas, I lost my super sleeping powers. I was unable to knock out in a moments notice. No longer did piles of rocks or ammo crates become appealing to me. My weak and tired body needed a soft and comfy bed with pillows. No longer would my Kevlar and rolled up ACU top suffice as a cushion for my head. Even with the creature comforts of my own room, bed, sweet blissful carpet I could not sleep. so there I was in the VA office talking to the psychiatrist about Marvel and DC movies. She looked just as tired and haggard as I was. She wore a top knot white coat with coffee stains, Marvel heroes t-shirt, green scrub bottoms, and a pair of dirty chucks—my kind of lady. She broke it down for me, Barney style, so that I could really grasp what was going on with me. I'm just happy she didn't pull out the crayons, but she insisted those were for a different group of service members. If I recall correctly, we are all born with about a 15% likelihood to have some kind of depression. That average increases about 25%–50% if one of your parents have ever had depression. Then, you add on a trauma, like war, that's another 25%-50% likelihood. So on the low end, there was 65% chance I was depressed, on the high end, a 115% chance I was fucked up. She told me that it would be crazy to come back from war without any issues. She also explained to me that with a lot combat veterans, our adrenaline, our "fight or flight" hormone has been set on overdrive for so long that it's very difficult to bring it back down. Combat vets were always hypervigilant in the sandbox, always at the ready, head on a swivel and never really being at ease because our life depended on our ability to effectively react to a dangerous situation. We don't need that kind of hypervigilance when we come home, but our brains have already been rewired to think this way. This hypervigilance made it difficult for some service members to sleep and affected other areas of their personal life. So what my doc wanted to do was to bring my adrenaline levels down, from a chemical standpoint. In other words, fighting fire with fire by prescribing me escitalopram, an antidepressant.

I got my stamp of approval for PTSD, a disability rating, drugs, and everything was going to be cake from there on out! Not exactly. I was going through a tough break up and had to move out because of it. I was working at a job that was an hour away from my mom's house, so thank you beautiful LA traffic for that. I was looking for a new place to live because as much as I love my ma, I can't live with her. She's going to hate that I wrote that in this book.

So I had a lot going on at that particular time in my life. At the same time, I was taking these antidepressants. I hated taking those drugs. Hell, I don't even smoke weed (I tried it once or twice), which I'd also been recommended to do, so to take antidepressants, I hated every second of them. If you've ever taken these drugs, you'll know what I mean. You become very lethargic, zombie-like even. You are there in real time but nothing can really get a reaction out of you. The concept of time is very slow and ambiguous. I was definitely calmer, so calm that friends and family could notice the difference in me. They said I wasn't really all there, the lights were on but nobody was home. It was very different for me because at times I tend to resemble a cute little puppy: furry, loving affection and attention, always the center of a party, easily excited, loved meeting new people so much that I would pee a little. However, on these drugs, the old me was nowhere to be found. I talked to a few fellow vets and they advised me to immediately get off of the meds. They had experienced the same reactions and were very adamant about tossing the drugs in exchange for a blunt. I stopped taking the pills. Maybe had I taken the pills for the amount of time I was medically recommended and stuck with it I'd have had a different reaction. I can't tell you to take or stop taking the antidepressants (my imaginary lawyers have advised against that), but what I can say is listen to your medical providers, listen to other vets in the same boat and find the method that works best for you. We are all different and deal with issues in a different manner. I can't say I've joined the United Cannabis Coalition, but I haven't written it off just yet.

Just like drugs and alcohol affect us all in a different way, so does PTSD. No one PTSD is alike, and this one was mine. I've touched on my sleeplessness, my moments of wanting to beat somebody into a bloody mess, my inability to open up emotionally, but there are a few other aspects of my PTSD I haven't covered yet. Now, I didn't get anger tantrums like a few of my fellow veterans, but I've had my outbursts of anger. Road rage was a big one for me. As soon as I hit the freeway, every other car was driven by some dumb motherfucker who didn't know how to drive or use a turn signal. I was constantly holding my hand out in disbelief as I questioned the driver's rationale when crossing all four lanes of the freeway, nearly hitting me. Worse even is when I ride my motorcycle and legally split lanes. California drivers, please, look before you merge and share the damn road! I can't tell how many birds I've flipped and how many head shakes of disapproval I've given to unaware drivers. I have good reason to though, having been hit three times on your bike puts a chip on your shoulder; it's not fun and my adrenaline always shoots through the roof. Yet, whenever I went down, I always had the same reaction: "Is my bike ok?" I could be limping with a broken leg and shattered collar bones and still be concerned about my bike's wellbeing. God forbid anything would happen my motorcycle, Beyoncé, I can't lose her.

Road rage wasn't the only symptom for me. I would get very anxious and nervous before speaking to people, which is odd because I'm normally very confident in public speaking, but I had a very good way of hiding my anxiety. I could feel the anxiety rumble beneath the surface as I confidently smiled, spoke, and laughed along with the group. This has improved greatly; now, I walk around like I own the place while shooting imaginary guns from the hip with a wink and smug grin on my face. Like everything else in life, this took time.

I've also had issues when it's come to nightmares, having trust issues in closed environments with a bunch of people I don't know. I was always very aware and always scanning the room, just in case anybody tried to pull some funny business. I would be prepared. Come on though, let's be real—the likelihood of that really happening is very slim, and we only look as crazy as we portray ourselves to be. My wife constantly tells me how crazy she is. Either she's lying or I've yet to make her reach that level of crazy yet. One word of advice: when you don't feel comfortable in a new place with new people, just dive in balls deep and engulf yourself in the unknown. Get to know people, look around, get up and walk around. Don't be the weird person in the corner of the room with shifty eyes. That won't get anyone to approach you, let alone screw you. Also, something I teach my students and take to heart—you need to get comfortable with being uncomfortable. Not everything will be as you once knew and not everything will be relatable. As my father once told me, the only constant in life is change.

PTSD comes in many forms and many situations, in my belief, it can even change or be exacerbated dependent upon different variables. For instance, I've never had a problem with fireworks after Afghanistan. I actually really enjoy watching them and being around friends and family. I once celebrated New Year's in Cusco, Peru, where fireworks are essentially flash grenades. I was pretty "lit" (as the cool kids say) myself. However, two years ago, during the Fourth of July celebrations, I was incredibly drunk. A real good kind of buzz. I had been drinking for hours straight at a hotel party. I was with my closest friends having a grand time and the fireworks were about to start. Now maybe it was different this time because of where I was in relation to the fireworks and the amount of alcohol I had consumed, but it was the most daunting Fourth of Julys I will ever remember. The hotel we were at was neighbored to Disneyland and they put on a good show every year. The first firework took off; a red stream followed a brilliant light into the sky. A thunderous crack struck and I was taken back to Afghanistan. I couldn't break away from the fireworks. I kept replaying images of the dead children and soldiers I cared for. The sounds of mortars and artillery replayed in my head. My friend, J, could tell something was off with me. She asked if I was okay. I didn't know how to respond but tears were rolling down my face. She was aware of my military service and I had shared my stories with her. She knew I was having a "moment." She said it would be okay, leaned her head on me, patted my back, and comforted me as best as she could. Thank you, J, you really did help me that night. I'm very grateful to have you in my life.

Oddly enough, I haven't had the same reactions to fireworks since that night. I'm just fine around them. Maybe it was a fluke, maybe I took one too many shots of tequila, but I would advise you to be mindful of mixing alcohol and PTSD. It may not always end in tragedy, but it's not all that fun either.

We all experience PTSD differently and we all need to find our own remedies for it. For some it's counseling, for others it's prescription drugs and some meditation. Whatever path is best for you, please, get help and don't fight this battle alone. I don't want to lose any more vets to suicide. I want to raise a cup with all of you again. I would love to see you all happy, successful, and in meaningful relationships. Even if the only person willing to listen to you has never been through what you have been through, take advantage of their kindness. A lot of people are willing to help if you only let them.

Suicide Numbers

I think people genuinely care a lot about veterans but may not have all the information needed to sustain this care for more than a Facebook post. Hopefully, some of this information will hit home for you. Hopefully, it will create new ideas for how to help veterans. I'm not asking you to start a non-profit, I'm not demanding you volunteer at a veterans outreach center, but maybe you'd be informed enough to vote for legislation that helps fund veteran needs. Help vote for those running for office that have a track record of helping vets and not just using them as political pawns. Or, you could help sway the minds of the Supreme Court Justices and urge them to hear the case of hundreds of veterans affected by open-air burn pits. Simple things like voting could go a long way. Now, I don't claim to know all the statistics or information related to veterans health, income, wellbeing, or other factors, but I hope to share bits of pieces of information that I did find very interesting. Hopefully, some of it will pique your interest and you can start to do some of your own research as well.

When it comes to the veteran community, there is nothing more concerning that veteran suicides. You may wonder why someone would succumb to the ultimate decision of taking their own life. It's not an easy decision to make, nor is it the first decision to be had. I believe that we all go through our own pains and battles in our own way. Sometimes we lose the war within ourselves and see suicide as the next step in defeat.

The thought of suicide has crossed my mind before. It was a short lived thought but it made me think of a few things. My issues might be resolved, but with my death, a wave new problems would rise up and come crashing down on everyone I've ever or would ever care about. Too many people depend on me and too many people depend on you too.

The findings and information in this chapter are provided by:

The VA National Suicide Data Report from 2005– 2016, a report released under the Office of Mental Health and Suicide Prevention in September of 2018.

"Suicide is the 10th leading cause of death in the United States, and veteran suicide is a national concern."

Here are the key points highlighted in their findings:

Veteran Suicides

"Veteran suicides per year decreased from 6,281 deaths in 2015 to 6,079 deaths in 2016. The number of Veteran suicides in 2016 remains greater than the 5,797 Veteran suicides that occurred in 2005. From 2015 to 2016, the Veteran population decreased by about 4 million people. Given that the Veteran population decreased in size, the number of Veteran suicides per year can also decrease even while the rate of Veteran suicide increases."

What does this mean? Well, essentially, although we can see a slight decrease in veteran suicides from 2015 to 2016, we can also see a decrease in the veteran population, which contributes to less suicides. Although the veteran population size has decreased, as a country we are still struggling to battle veteran suicides.

Veteran Suicide Rates

"VA examined rates of suicide among Veterans and non-Veteran adults in the United States. Unadjusted, or crude rates are helpful for understanding mortality within each population. In 2016, the unadjusted suicide rate among Veterans was 30.1 per 100,000, while the rate among non-Veteran adults was 16.4 per 100,000. However, when making comparisons, it is important to adjust for differences in population age and gender, as the Veteran population is older and has a higher percentage of men compared to the non-Veteran population. In 2016, the age-and gender-adjusted rates of suicide were 26.1 per 100,000 for Veterans and 17.4 per 100,000 for non-Veteran adults. Suicide rates for both Veterans and non-Veteran adults increased between 2005 and 2016."

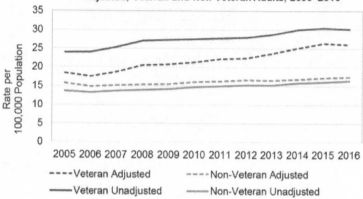

This is great news, it may not be a huge decrease but any lives saves is better than no lives saved. Sadly, the overall suicide rates for veterans and non-veteran adults have increased from 2005 to 2016. There is something going on in our society where suicide seems to be more prevalent—it's not just one issue, nor is it because we are raising kids to be weak. There are mountains of obstacles that I could not even begin to try and address. I just hope more research is done to help those in need. Lastly, it does make sense that veterans are 1.5 times more likely to commit suicide than non-veteran adults. It's not that non-veterans don't experience trauma—lots of people do and I would never try to downplay that trauma. However, war is an ugly world, and in it you see, live, and experience the ugliest side of man. Once, in basic training, my drill instructor, SSG. B, asked us why we had joined. One recruit answered that he read that one could "find themselves in war." SSG. B laughed at him and said he'd find himself shitting his pants and that was the stupidest reason to want to go to war, let alone join the military. He explained how no one should ever want to go to war but that they should be prepared to go.

Veteran Suicide Methods

"Among methods used in attempting suicide, firearms are associated with the highest rate of suicide mortality. In 2016, 69.4 percent of Veteran suicides and 48.4 percent of non-Veteran adult suicides resulted from a firearm injury. Among Veterans, in 2016 70.6 percent of male suicide deaths and 41.2 percent of female suicide deaths resulted from a firearm injury. Interventions focused on preventing self-harm by firearm are integral to preventing Veteran suicide."

It's sad to think that this comes as no surprise that overall, 69.4% of veterans commit suicide by way of firearm. A lot of veterans, including myself, own or have access to guns, so that makes the task much easier. Poisoning, which may or may not include drug overdoses (this study was not specific in regards to drug overdose), is at 10.6%, Suffocation is at 15%, and Other is at 5.1%. I don't even want to imagine what "Other" entails. I'll say this about guns—regardless if you are for guns, against guns, or somewhere in the middle, if you know someone dealing with thoughts of hurting themselves or others, have that difficult discussion about reliving them of their weapons, at least until they seek medical and professional help.

One statistic that jumps out at me is the huge difference in male veteran and female veteran suicide rates. Male veterans have a suicide rate of 70.6% while the female veteran has a suicide rate of 41.2%. That's almost a 30% difference! Why would this be? I honestly don't know, but I could make a few assumptions you may or may not agree with. I believe that within the U.S., women are encouraged to express their feelings more, or it is at least more acceptable for women to express their feelings and talk about what bothers them. Now, not all women may fall into this category, but I'd wager money that women have a better sense of emotional intelligence than men. This isn't to say men can't have emotional intelligence, but we may find it later on in life. Men are generally taught to "suck it up," "don't let them see you cry," and to "be a man." There is a huge stereotype men are faced with having to live up to, and at times, we men believe that any emotion is weakness. As a result, we are less likely to talk about our problems or open up to those willing to listen. When you can't or won't open up about what's eating at you, it can eventually swallow you whole.

Veteran Suicides by Age Group

"The suicide rate among Veterans ages 18–34 increased substantially in recent years, and the rate in 2016 was significantly higher than in 2014 (Figure 4). Rates of suicide are highest among younger male Veterans ages 18–34 and lowest among male Veterans ages 55–74 (Figure 6). Despite the increased suicide rate among Veterans ages 18–34, Veterans ages 55–74 represented the greatest share of suicide deaths in 2016, with Veterans age 55 and older accounting for 58.1 percent of suicide deaths."

Two big takeaways for me when it comes to age. First, I fall into the increased suicide rates for veterans 18-34 years of age—45 per 100,000. It's daunting to think that so many young veterans have been taking their lives at such an alarming rate. Why has this increased? Where is the mentorship a lot of the younger veterans need? I guess I can't just say that it's because of a lack of leadership, but that could be a contributing factor. When I say "leadership," I don't just mean the military chain of command or older veterans; anyone who is older and has more years of experience can be a mentor. To be honest, you don't even have to be older—I've mentored people far beyond my years because I was in a position of authority and experience. I'm sure we've all ran into some of the younger folks who looked lost in the sauce, and we could have guided them, but instead said, "They need to figure it out for themselves." I'm not sure that's always the right answer, because not everyone learns the same way. I'd say, in the future, if you are ever presented with an opportunity to mentor someone, even if for a moment, take it. You'll feel rewarded that you helped mold someone into a better person and you'll be engrained into them for the rest of their lives, leaving a bit of legacy behind. What's better than leaving your mark on this world?

Another aspect of this particular section of the study is that veterans aged 55 and older make up 58.1% of the veteran suicides. Is this the opposite effect of the younger veterans? Did we forget or ignore our more seasoned veterans? Did we stop listening to their stories and stop appreciating them for their service and for their age? Maybe. Maybe there is more to this that is yet to be uncovered. If there's one thing I enjoy doing is swapping war stories with older vets. You can see their younger selves again, their pride shines and they have that twinkle in their eye again. The older vets I've spoken with have genuinely liked talking about their time in the service and they've also opened up and unloaded what they've held onto for so many years. One time, when I was working at a civilian hospital as a patient administrator; I started talking to this old Italian patient. He learned that I was in the service and we chatted for about a half an hour after his appointment. He'd been in WWII and seen some shit. He was describing how he was a .50 caliber gunner on either a tank or a jeep. In the middle of his story he gets to the part where he describes how he "cut a Kraut in half with my .50 cal." His laughing stopped, he became somber, looked me dead in the eyes and said, "That was the first time I ever killed a man." He began to cry and was very emotional. He thanked me for the time spent and apologized for crying and left. I was left very emotional too and his stories weighed on me. I began to wonder, would I become like him one day? I like to think by just listening to this old *Italiano*, I was able to help him let some of that pain out. I hope he found a little more peace that night.

I think our older veterans really enjoy sharing their stories about the military whenever they can. I challenge you to shoot the shit with an old vet. It doesn't have to be just about war, but it could be about the military in general. Hear their stories about how they fucked around just as much as we did during their service. Listen to the stories of how they would get shitty drunk with their mates, how they were one mean motherfucker, how they hated their chain of command too, how they miss the old days, how they miss their friends, and above all, listen to the advice they have to give. Learn the lessons that come with age; these are precious moments. It's like seeing into the future, and at most, it might cost you a beer or a smoke.

Suicide Among Veterans Who Use the Veteran Health Administration (VHA)

"VA examined the suicide count and rates among Veterans who recently used VHA care and Veterans who did not use VHA care. Veterans who recently used VHA are defined as Veterans who had a VHA encounter in the calendar year of death or in the previous year. After adjusting for age, the suicide rate among Veterans who recently used VHA was higher than among Veterans who did not (Figure 7). However, between 2005 and 2016, among Veterans who were not in VHA care, the percentage increase (26.0 percent) in the suicide rate was greater than the percentage increase (13.7 percent) in the rate among Veterans in VHA care. This is similar to information presented in the previous report and is consistent with findings reported elsewhere. Veterans who use VHA have physical and mental health care needs and are actively seeking care because those conditions are causing disruption in their lives. Many of these conditions — such as mental health challenges, substance use disorders, chronic medical conditions, and chronic pain — are associated with an increased risk for suicide."

This was a scary figure to process. veterans receiving care from the VHA had an increased suicide rate of 13.7%. Yet, for those not seeking VHA care, suicide rates increased to 26%. I hate to say it, but it feels like damned if you do and damned if you don't. I know there is a lot of hate that falls on the VA healthcare system. Could they be better? Sure. Could they figure out a more productive way of taking care of our veterans? I have no doubt in my mind. But I honestly believe that those working in the VA healthcare system truly want to help us out. I've been fortunate enough to not wait years for disability rating (it did take 10 months though) like some of my fellow vets. Wait times have been hit or miss with me. Some are rather accommodating and others, not so merciful. Yet, you have to take into consideration the high volume departments veterans are being seen in. Mental Health is always packed, Auditory seems to be just as busy. I was sent to outside clinics as well. I really hope the VA can get some leadership that cuts away some of that red tape that prevents the good folks at the VA from really being able to help us vets out. You can see the pain and disappointment in the eyes of the VA workers when they have to turn you away or can't process your "paperwork" because you still have three other forms to fill out and get verified by another department. I found the VA workers to be very empathetic to veteran needs (many of them being veterans themselves), which is why they would try to help by giving you time saving information or tactics to use on your medical journey. I think the folks at the VA really do care, there is just a lot of us that they're trying to care for.

Woman Veteran Suicides

"VA examined the suicide count and rate among women Veterans. Between 2005 and 2016, woman Veteran suicide counts increased, as did the woman Veteran population (Figures 8 and 9). After adjusting for differences in age, the rate of suicide among women Veterans was higher than the rate among non-Veteran women (Figure 10). The woman Veteran suicide rate decreased from 2015 to 2016, but the difference was not statistically significant."

Fellow veterans, don't forget about our sisters who could be secretly hurting as well. Although it is true that there are less women veterans committing suicide versus their male counterparts; that doesn't mean we should be less concerned. Even just one woman veteran suicide is one too many. I've heard of and seen women veteran groups at school and through the VA that focus on the care for women veterans. I think it's great to offer that to women veterans because there are things that a woman veteran might have had to endure that I didn't because I'm a man. Let's be honest, women veterans still deal with rape and sexual harassment while in the service. Sometimes those encounters leave lifelong scars. I've met a few while working at LRMC. I would go to the psych wards to collect patient documents for medical records and would see the ladies there. At times, I would wheel them into the ER as they were unloaded off the buses. I'd overhear the doctors and nurses pulling out rape kits. It's disheartening to know that some of us can't look passed skin and flesh and see a fellow warrior. Sure, we get froggy back in the barracks, but if it's not consensual, it's not okay. Don't be that guy or girl.

Former Guard and Reserve Service Member Suicides

"Between 2005 and 2016, the suicide count increased for former Service members who were never federally activated National Guard and Reserve members. National Guard and Reserve members may not have Veteran legal status due to their type of service. This can limit their access to VA benefits and services under current laws and regulations. In partnership with the DoD, VA now operates a mobile Vet Center to increase Guard and Reserve members' access to mental health care. Further expansion of suicide prevention activities for the former Guard and Reserve population is planned for fiscal year 2019."

This may be a surprise, but it's not really if you think about it. Just because a service member has not been to war does not mean they have not experienced some kind of trauma. Their basic training could have been traumatic or they could have been abused, raped, or had a really shitty command or job that squeezed the joy out of their lives. We all experience things differently and cope with them in different ways. What might have been easy for me might have been the hardest test of someone else's life. We can't judge those if we've never walked in their shoes or looked through their eyes and we shouldn't. We are all different and have different levels of tolerance and risk.

If you ever think of committing suicide, please do me one favor and try to look past yourself. Who would you be hurting by doing this? Someone would be effected. Someone would be saddened and pained by you no longer being in this world. Family, friends, colleagues, classmates, lovers, those whose lives you've touched, the people you smile and wave to on your way to work, the person you've reached out to in their time of need, and the countless souls you have yet to reach out and embrace. Suicide affects all of us, not just you. I truly believe all humans are connected to one another. I can't explain how but can see it and feel it. I can think of two examples that let me know we are all connected. Think about the how you felt when someone has passed away. Remember how much it hurt? How your insides cramped up, your throat dried and you could barely breathe because the pain was just too much to bare? You felt every second of that passing and no amount of booze, condolences, or hugs could ease your aching heart. Another time we feel a real connection is at the birth of a child. The baby doesn't even have to be yours but you are happy. You see the world in that child's eyes. For a second, your hopes and dreams are brought back to surface again and you want nothing more than that newborn baby, to have every opportunity granted to them. Everyone surrounding that child is happier, at ease, warm, and hopeful. I'm sure these feelings are even stronger for the parents. Maybe one day I'll know what it feels like to welcome my own child into this world. Until that day comes, I hope I can reach you and help you make a better decision than suicide. Hopefully I can inspire you to help someone else in need. We all need each other.

Extra Stats

Here are a few extra stats to curb your statistical hunger. Why am I shoving more stats down your throat? To be honest, I don't think a lot of you will research this information on your own unless you have a class project or get paid to research such information. I'm guilty of this as well. Let's be honest, looking up statistics isn't the most thrilling pastime, even if it's for a cause we care about. So, since I have your attention here, I'm hoping to take advantage of this opportunity and share some information you may not have been aware of before. Perhaps the more we inform others, the more people will become aware of the veterans community struggles so that more can be done to care for our fellow veterans.

Want to know a secret about me? One thing that truly terrifies and even gives me anxiety when I'm exposed to it, is seeing homeless people. An immense fear runs down my back and a wide range of thoughts and emotions run through my mind. No, it's not because homeless people themselves freak me out. It's not that I don't care or have empathy for them. It's because of the honest truth that any one of us can fall down that road and end up where they are. Whenever we see homeless people, what are the typical assumptions we make? They're lazy, on drugs, probably some gang banger or that's just how they want to live. We avoid eye contact and look the other way when they approach us asking for money. I think we make up these assumptions and choose to not acknowledge homeless people as people, because otherwise it would mean there was a connection to the passerby. If we look at a homeless person long enough, we begin to see ourselves in that person. We begin to imagine what it must be like to panhandle for money, live in a cardboard box, and not be able to properly bathe, eat, or relieve yourself as the rest of society does. The kicker to this is when I find out that same guy asking for cash is a Vietnam or Desert Storm vet. I look into their eyes and I wonder, is this my future, too? God, I hope not.

Let's break down some numbers:

Homelessness

The majority of homeless veterans are males

with roughly 9% being female. 11% of the homeless population are veterans. 45% of homeless veterans are Hispanic or African American, while only making up 10.4% and 3.4% of the of the veteran population. 9% of veterans are between the ages of 18-31, 41% are between the ages of 31-50. 1.4 million veterans are at risk of homelessness (Veterans, 2018). Approximately 12,700 veterans of OEF (Operation Enduring Freedom), OIF (Operation Iraqi Freedom), and OND (Operation New Dawn) were homeless in 2010. Over 40,000 veterans currently find themselves homeless. 25,000 veterans are living in temporary living facilities. 15,000 veterans are left without reliable shelter. 2018 was the first year we saw an increase in the homeless veteran population since 2010 (III, 2017).

It's scary to see these numbers. There are so many homeless veterans that it's unfathomable to understand how this happened. Why did we get some many homeless vets on the streets? Didn't the military provide training and counseling for these service members returning home? Didn't the VA do everything in its power to care for these warriors after the war? So many questions come to mind, and I wish I had the answers here, but all I can do is help you become aware of this widespread catastrophe.

Want to know why I'm so afraid of being homeless? I was almost there once. In my younger years, I had not developed the discipline to really have a savings. I had a good job and partied like a rock star. It was enough to get me by every two weeks and afford my car, rent, bills, and fun, but never really enough to save, at least with the spending habits I had at the time. Like all good parties, it eventually had to end. I was laid off from said good job with a few hundred dollars in my checking account, a car note due, and rent to pay. Well, fuck.

I ended up living on my dad's couch while I was looking for work. It sucked, it was definitely a low point in my life but it could have been worse. I could have been on the streets like plenty of other vets. I could have been that broken warrior, roaming the streets, looking for loosen change and scraps of food.

Disabilities

You know, it never occurred to me that I would have any kind of disability after leaving the army. It really never dawned on me but I guess that's what basic training does to you. We've all had that Superman mentality after basic training where we think we're indestructible, that no harm could ever come to us. Our drill sergeants did a good job of planting that seed in our heads. Yet, coming home after would be a different story. Some of our disabilities would be more plain to see than others, their scars hidden behind smiles and jokes. In 2017 alone, 4,552,804 had received some kind of disability rating. Of that total, 1,327,452 veterans received a rating of 0%–20%, 787,108 veterans received a rating of 30%–40%, 700,111 veterans received a rating of 50%–60%; 1,128,11 veterans received a rating of 70%–90%, and 609,322 veterans received a rating of 100% (Department of Veterans Affairs, 2017).

That's a lot of veterans to take care of, and if I'm being honest, I'd say there is probably a lot more than that. The reason I say that is because I'm sure many of you, like myself, have said, "Well, I came back with all my fingers and toes, but Joe over there, that fucking guy lost his legs, he needs the disability more than me." I'm here to tell you, that is the wrong way to look at it. Yes, Joe lost his legs and that is horrible, but you can't compare one person's injury or trauma to another. We all have different tolerances and we all deal with different kinds of pains. You can't see scars on someone with PTSD, rape doesn't leave trauma marks on it's victims, and you can't see the thoughts of suicide that run through that young private's mind when he finds out his wife cheated on him, while deployed overseas.

I'm not taking anything away from those who have lost limbs or senses, but you should never discount yourself or your injuries, whether physical or not. If you are hurting and think, "maybe I should talk to someone," go to the VA and start your process as soon as you can.

It took me six years, after the military to consider going to the VA and I wish I would have gone sooner. Maybe I could have prevented some of the mistakes I had or at least led a more productive life earlier on. I could have applied for other benefits a lot sooner and not let so much time pass by before realizing I needed a change. Don't be like me and wait. Get yourself checked out, head to toe, and if you're entitled to benefits, take full advantage of them and tell others to do the same.

Criminal Activity

Oddly enough, for a group of people that have been reconditioned to follow orders, obey rules, and not so much as fart without asking for permission, quite a few of us have had our run-ins with the law. I know I have. Upon my arrival home from war, nothing kept me better company than sex and alcohol. I think I was drinking my sorrows away and fucking the war out of me. I was never into drugs, but alcohol and promiscuous sex sure filled the void when my emotional tank was running on empty, and during that part of my life, I was always running on empty. Well, all that drinking eventually caught up to me in the form of a DUI. It's no fun being drunk as shit and sleeping on a slab of concrete in a freezing, air-conditioned room with nothing but an orange jumpsuit to keep you warm. The food I was given was shit. MREs would have been a godsend. I choked down some white bread, tossed back a milk carton, and cuddled with the only heat source I had—the crappy excuse of spaghetti wrapped in saran wrap. I laid my head down on the comfort of cement, closed my eyes, saw the spinning stars, and drifted off to a tequila-induced slumber.

Yet, I'm sure my midnight tale of an Orange County jail cell is not uncommon. I'd wager a few of you reading have similar stories.

In December of 2015, the Bureau of Justice Statistics released some incredible findings about veteran incarceration percentages. The overall good news is that less and less veterans have been going to jail. In 2004 there were 203,000 incarcerated veterans, and since then we've seen that number decrease to 181,500 (8% of all inmates in state, federal and local jails) from 2011–2012 (Jennifer Bronson, 2015).

If we take a closer look at the numbers we can see the breakdown of the kind of veterans that end up behind bars. With the numbers provided, the incarceration rate is about 855 per 100,000 veterans, which is a lower rate than nonveterans, who make up about 968 per 100,000. Two-thirds of veterans in prison (67%) and jail (66%) were discharged from the military between 1974–2000. veterans who were discharged during OEF, OIF, and OND accounted for 13% of veterans in prison and 25% of veterans in jail between 2011–2012. About half of the veterans in prison (48%) and jail (55%) have been diagnosed with a mental health disorder (Jennifer Bronson, 2015).

One major stat that stood out to me, reported by Quil Lawrence of NPR, was that 99% of the incarcerated veterans between 2011–2012 were men (Lawrence, 2015)! Holy shit, guys, 99% is bananas. By that same token, well done, ladies, well done. So what is it that creates such a huge, disparaging gap between men and women with incarceration rates? I'm definitely curious about this. Are men more prone to breaking the law that women? I'd say so—in the total population, 93% of inmates are males (Prisons, 2018).

Well, men, we could definitely learn a thing or two from our female counterparts. I'm not going to pretend to understand the psychological differences in male and female psyches and why men are more prone to going to jail, but it sounds like it's worth looking into. In order to solve a problem, we have to admit that there is one, and from the looks of it, guys, we have a big problem.

Overall, as sad as it is to see so many brother and sisters behind bars, it brings me great comfort that those incarceration rates have been on the decline for a while now. However, I think this begs the question: why are veterans being locked up to begin with? Ms. Sheena Rice of the News Bureau of the University of Missouri wrote an interesting article based off the work of Ms. Kelli Canada, an assistant professor of social work at MU (Rice, 2017). In Rice's article, Canada explains that there are three meaningful themes that were apparent in her interviews with veterans. One that comes to no surprise is *alcohol and drug use.* Alcohol and drug use was shown to be exacerbated by trauma in the military. I'm sure a lot of us (myself included) self-medicate to keep the horror at bay. Canada also lists *difficulty adjusting to civilian life.* This is too damn true. A lot of us come out of the military not really knowing what the hell to do. Partly, I think it's because we're so used to having someone tell us what to do, where to do it, and how to properly execute it. We're on our own in the civilian world and don't have a drill sergeant or NCO's hand to hold. Along with this, Canada mentions that we veterans have a difficult time finding "meaningful" work after the military. I can attest to this. Now, I think there is a huge difference between finding a burger flipping job (no offense to anyone working fast food restaurants or my younger sister who currently works under the golden arches) and a "meaningful," or I like to think a comparable, job to what we had in the military. Take yours truly, for example: I was in an E-7 slot as an E-5 NCOIC of the Patient Administration Department. I was in charge of that department and made sure proper reports were distributed to higher command, patient data was collected, statistical analyses was provided, training was given, department practices were improved and supporting staff was taken care of. I did a lot in that job but ask me if I can do that in the civilian side? A lot of us veterans were given tons of responsibility and did incredible work, but unfortunately, it doesn't really transfer over to civilian work. We still need a piece of paper that says we can do the job we have years of experience doing. It's a kick in the balls to realize all that you did in the military doesn't mean shit when you get out.

That brings us to Canada's third theme, which I believe ties into the second theme—*economic disadvantages*. If we can't get a job, we can't pay the bills, simple as that. Even a minimum wage job won't cut it with rent, bills, utilities, gas, insurance, and food. We end up homeless and on the streets asking for a few bucks to get a bite to eat. Also, some of us joined the military right out of high school, so we never had to pay rent, balance a checkbook, or really understand how credit actually works. It's not like the military mandates classes on how to prepare for the real world, financially at least (hint, hint, U.S. military). We get told, "Don't slap the dog and don't kick your wife." In some aspects, we are still children when we get out of the military, child soldiers that understand flanking and how best to kill a target 300 yards away but don't have a good handle on finances and meaningful relationships that allow us to express ourselves emotionally. That stuff, you need to figure out on your own. So we know what gets us into jail, but what has been keeping us out of jail? What has been helping that number steadily decline after so many years? Well, I'd wager the access to medical services such as the VA has played a part, and well as educational and vocational services for veterans, along with outreach programs targeting homeless veterans. In today's society, we've seen a lot of programs that are aimed at helping out veterans when they return home. Let's be honest, coming home isn't always the end of our war torn struggles; it could very well be the beginning of them.

I've received assistance myself from groups such as Working Wardrobes in Irvine, CA. I took an IT class there that they offer free for veterans, and they also have lots of companies and organizations that are always trying to find work for veterans. Granted, some of these jobs may not be the blue- or white-collar jobs we would all hope for, but it's a place to get you going in the right direction.

I really hope that the information I provided you in this chapter helps you become more aware of veterans and their struggles. Just hearing about veterans doesn't seem to be as impactful, so hopefully if we can associate people with numbers that directly correlate to the reality veterans face, it might grease the hamster wheel in more people's heads. Like G.I. Joe says, "knowing is half the battle."

From Hip-pocket Training to University

Get some training, you lazy fuck!

In the military, you've spent an entire career training and learning. Granted, they may not have been the most stimulating of topics, but they kept your brain working. When we leave the military, a good majority of us veterans become complacent. It's hard to be motivated when you don't have a senior enlisted NCO screaming at you to be at the motor pool at 0600 hours for "training." And no, he doesn't give a shit if your MOS is supply, you'll be turning wrenches just like all the other grease monkeys.

So, why all the training? To be honest, it's to keep us trouble makers from breaking something or ending up in sick call. I'm sure parents can relate to this. You know, you give your kids a "job" to do in hopes of giving you a few moments of peace before resorting to violence and criminal charges—yup, just like that. Soldiers, just like all other service members, have a natural act for doing stupid shit. Don't know why, but that's just the way it is. (I have a theory that the military puts something in the water buffalos.)

During basic training, we not only learn our basic soldiering skills but a few other items that come in handy as well—training themes such as first aid, basic combat lifesaving, survival training, land navigation (which everyone sucks at), and how to survive a nuclear blast by laying on the floor, tummy side down, with your helmet digging into the dirt as it shields you from the blast. In the rare occasion that soldiers have any down time, drill instructors will command all recruits to pull out their "Army Field Training Manuals." This is a handy dandy book that fits in your cargo pocket and travels with you everywhere. This is commonly referred to as "hip-pocket training." So, as the drill sergeants have to set up a rifle range, attend to a particular soldier, or are awaiting another platoon to join up, soldiers are expected to pull out their field manuals and train by reading. This manual is considered our bible. It has all the do's and don'ts of the Army along with useful information on how to adorn ribbons and rank, the soldier's creed, your three general orders, ranking structure, and a whole slew of information I have repressed in order to keep my sanity. Bottom line, in Basic Combat Training, you have no reason to find yourself dicking around, especially when you have a thesaurus thick book with everything you would ever need to know. What's really funny is that after basic training, you forget about the field manual. It probably collects dust somewhere in a box or on top of a book case, but I always smile in remembrance when I see a platoon of ROTC kids standing at parade rest, holding a field manual to their face.

So then, what happens when we get out of the military? Do we continue training? Do we continue to PT? A lot of us don't continue those rituals anymore. Why? We finally get a break from it all. After the years of abuse we put our bodies through and the relentless bullshit training we've had to endure, enough is enough and we need a break. Yet, that's all we should allow ourselves, just a break. I'm not saying we don't deserve more time to process, but I believe that the military was always trying to teach us how to grow and become stronger, smarter, and more effective. Sadly, when we depart from the military, that forced sense of accountability goes out the window as soon as we put our feet up on the coffee table and sip on a nice cold lager. We begin to justify to ourselves that we don't need PT, we don't need "training," we did our time, fuck that jazz, but I think it's a step off the cliff to go cold turkey from it all.

Think about it—we have been conditioned to always be training, always keeping ourselves mentally and physically fit. Then, when we leave the military, we just stop? You don't think there could be any repercussions with that decision? The same reason we should continue to work out and keep our minds stimulated are the same reasons our drill sergeants kept us busy with PT and hip-pocket training: to keep our asses out of trouble. Whether it's been a few months or a few years since you said your farewells to the military, it'd behoove you to start your path on some form of education. Now, what kind of education should you pursue? That depends on you and what benefits you have available, but I implore you, get back to school, training, trades... anything that will help you grow and reach new levels of achievement. Lucky for you, in the good 'ol U.S. of A, you have choices to fulfill your educational needs and desires.

Now, let me throw out a disclaimer: I am not a professional educational advisor (not quite), nor do I know all the details to all the veteran benefits available to you. All I can do is share with you what benefits I have used and researched on my own.

First things first, figure out what educational or vocational benefits you have. You can go to **https://benefits.va.gov/gibill/** or call 1-888-GIBILL-1 to find out what benefits you have. However, be patient when calling, and I mean be very patient. I've been on hold for more than an hour while waiting for someone to pick up the phone. I get it, there's a lot of us vets, but Jesus, Mary, and Joseph, hire more folks, I'm talking to you, VA! Also, if you've scored a disability rating of 10% or higher (ratings could change in the future) and were discharged with honorable or other than honorable, you might be eligible for Vocational Rehabilitation (Chapter 31). What's Voc Rehab you say? It's not educational benefits. Repeat after me: "Voc Rehab is not educational benefits." Please understand this and don't screw it up when you try to claim Voc Rehab benefits. Voc Rehab is for "vocational" (work) training. It's designed to get your ass into a job. The end goal is to get you to work, not to send you to school, that's what the G.I Bill is for. Now, having said that, if you can avoid it, don't use up all of your G.I Bill housing benefits as you can roll those benefits over to Voc Rehab.

Now, you first have to apply through your eBenefits account. If you don't have an account, go to: **https://www.ebenefits.va.gov/ebenefits/homepage** and set one up. Once you start the Voc Rehab process and have a date to interview, don't be late and don't reschedule. I've heard of veterans being told "sorry, no benefits for you because you missed the date." Other vets were lucky and were able to reschedule, but do you really want to chance it? You'll have to fill out lots of forms and provide a lot of details. Also, be sure to have a career/job goal in mind. Do some research on it and see if it's relatable to your previous training, education, or MOS—this will come in handy. One final warning: your benefits are in the hands of your Voc Rehab counselor, so don't be a dick because they can deny you your benefits. Stick to the program—go to school/training, and get your career started.

Whichever route you take—G.I Bill, Voc Rehab, or both—you need to do your due diligence on what educational/training institute you'll be going to. Don't expect the counselors to know everything; it's up to you to know what you want and what path you need to take. Use me as an example.

I previously used my G.I bill to go to community college and got my AST in Business Administration. When I got my disability rating, I found out that I could get additional vocational benefits too. So, I signed up and had a meeting with my one-day Voc Rehab counselor, which took me 8 months get the appointment. He was a nice enough guy and very friendly. However, I think in his attempt to "square me away," he dropped the ball. (I'll explain a bit later.)

I enjoy the business side of the world but also love how technology helps businesses make those informed decisions. I had used data, technology and information in the past and thought: Technology! It's the way of the future! Maybe I'd like IT work or Computer Networking, that sounds cool! I explained to my Voc Rehab counselor that I would really like to get a job in Computer Networking. He seemed very happy to hear about my ambitions. A few clicks on his keyboard and he said, "Okay, you're all set, you'll be going to Cal State Fullerton and getting a bachelors in Computer Networking." My mouth dropped, I was stunned. Just like that? Just like that I was going to school, all expenses paid, and getting a bachelor's degree!? I was so happy and overwhelmed with joy that I couldn't stop thanking him. I had always wanted to finish school but never had the money (also didn't make it a priority). So, here I was, going to be a college kid at 32 years old. I texted my then girlfriend (now wife) and she was super happy for me. When it dawned on her that she was dating a college kid, we laughed about it. But as I was enrolling in school at CSUF, I came to a harrowing realization: CSUF did not offer a bachelor's degree in Computer Networking… but my counselor said… Fuck. No such degree existed at CSUF, and I had to elect a major in order to enroll, so I chose Computer Science. After getting accepted and understanding what computer science entailed, I realized that was not the subject for me. I had a few buddies in the field and they suggested that I might be a better fit for Information Systems under the Business Administration Department. I went back to my original counselor to ask him to change my major/career goals, but lo and behold, he was no longer at the center where I signed up for my Voc Rehab benefits; he was gone. Then, I found out my file was being moved to West LA. I was left pissing in the wind. Eventually, with a few choicely-worded emails and advice from the veterans resource center at CSUF, I was able to switch over my major and start my path to a better career.

I could have avoided a lot of headaches had I done my own research and not just trusted the "pros." However, I'm happy to report that school is going amazing. I'm enjoying the college life and making tons of new friends. At CSUF we have a veterans Resource Center. It's a great place to hang out with other vets, get services, and join clubs. I really am enjoying my time at CSUF. It's been a long time coming.

Now, I'm going to a state school in California, but that's not the only option. Also, I understand that not everyone wants to spend two to four years in school. I get it, at times studies wear down on me too and I get a bit antsy. You can also use your benefits for apprenticeships, trade schools, credential programs, and certifications. However, whatever program you choose, make sure they are credentialed and their certifications actually have weight to them. Full disclosure, I teach at a for-profit school. Now, do I think the prices of tuition to take my courses are ridiculous? I sure do, but do I also think they serve a growing need? They definitely do. As a country, we need to realize the value of training and education that are found outside the walls of a university. We still need plumbers, HVAC technicians, medical billers, dental technicians, carpenters, welders, machinists, and a huge variety of other trades. I don't see a robot plumber coming to unclog my toilet anytime soon.

However, heed my warning, seeker of knowledge, not all schools are the same! Make sure you know what career you are aiming for and then find the course/school that will best serve your ambitious goals. Again, ensure that they are accredited, talk to past and current students, research reviews of that institution, and for the love of god, don't just blow your benefits on some easy training that you never plan on using just so you can pay your rent and have extra drinking money. Maximize the most out of your educational and vocational benefits. Make sure that you are getting more than just the ability to pay your rent. These are tools to help uplift that you are entitled to. Don't for a second think that you don't deserve these benefits. How many years did you give up on your dreams and your life to serve in the military? How many times did you say that "next year I'll…" and never did squat about it? How bad did it hurt when you thought someone wouldn't amount to shit in life and all of a sudden they're in a better place than you are? That's a straight uppercut to our pride. Stop putting your life off, and take advantage of what is owed to you and don't let anyone tell you different. I really hope you look into education and or training but these aren't the only options you have available to you either.

Did you know that the VA can also provide you a pathway to starting your own business? The VA has great information that gives you insight and a guide to creating or growing your own business, check out **https://www.va.gov/osdbu/entrepreneur/** to learn more about it.

I never thought that I could build my own business. I was never given the groundwork or vision to do so, not until I was 31 years old and was introduced to a photographer. I had always had a passion for photography—in reality, I just didn't want to forget all the things I had seen and done when I turned into a grumpy old vet, yelling at kids to "stay off my lawn"! One day, I was asked to tag along on a shoot and was handed a camera. Turns out, I had a natural eye for photography, and this motivated me to pursue a business in photography. So, I did. That's when **www.gbgphotographyca.com** was born. It's an amazing feeling to see something you have built continuously grow and give other people happiness. I also love the fact that now people recognize me as a professional photographer, admire work and look to me for expert advice. Who would have thought that this vet, who was always told to "go to school and get a good job" could start their own business? Creating a business takes a lot of dedication and willingness to acknowledge failure, and being able to adapt and grow. When you start your own business, you see yourself begin to change and evolve. You become more aware of the world by being more observant, you appreciate others' opinions a little bit more and you begin to mentor others as well. Mentorship itself is a very rewarding feeling, even if there is no immediate monetary gain from it. As much as I encourage anyone to continue their education and training, I also encourage you all to fuel that entrepreneurial spirit.

There a lots of ways to continuously grow and become more than what we are; we can find our higher calling through education, training, or entrepreneurship. Yet, you won't find enlightenment by sitting at that same depressing bar with the same bunch of Angry Veterans that continuously bitch and moan that things are never going to get better. Don't fall into the circle of stagnation as the rest of your friends and family look for improvement. On the same token, don't compare your successes and failures to anyone else. Only you can truly hold ownership of what you create or destroy, what you find or abandon, what you nurture or let die. I truly hope that all of you find the motivation you seek to put a fire in your belly and a boot in your ass. Don't worry if you don't know where the road less traveled will take you. It's an adventure, after all, and I'm positive you didn't know where life in the military would have taken you either. I implore you to never stop growing, never stop learning, and never stop changing your world. As the great Greek philosopher Heraclitus once said, "Change is the only constant in life."

You best be ready for that change.

Body & Mind

There are few things that help keep the fire from running wild within me—some have worked and some are absolutely ridiculous and have no benefit to me, whatsoever. Yet, what doesn't work for me may work for another. We are all hardwired differently and we are all affected differently, kind of like how we are all affected by war. What I saw and experienced can be a walk in the park for some, and others could be rendered into an emotional, vegetative state. It all depends on how we process our trauma and how we attempt to mitigate the pain left by that same trauma. I've picked up a few tricks along the way to self-healing that have seemed to work for me. What I have learned is not a cure-all, but it helps channel my anger and understand that though it is a part of me, I am the one in control and not the other way around. Hopefully, some of these methods can help combat the rage and sorrow that fuels the angry veteran in you.

For one, PT is still free. Just because we left the military doesn't completely excuse us from exercise. However, that doesn't mean you have to wake up at 0500 and report to a field with 10 other sleepy, grumpy, and annoyed veterans just to get some good old fashioned PT in. I'm thankful that I still exercise on a regular basis; it's a habit that never left me. Now, I'm not training to be an Olympic athlete or some Instagram chiseled "bro," but I want to live an active and semi-healthy lifestyle. I just don't want to end up old as shit with the inability to wipe my own ass. Also, I like it when I hop out of the shower and my wife darts me those 'fuck me' eyes as soon as I come swinging into the bedroom. As much as I enjoy my wife being grabby all over me, exercise is a great way for me to deal with stress and anxiety. Ever since Afghanistan, it has seemed like I get stressed and anxious more often than I used to. It's not a visible stress, but it's subtle, just beneath the surface. I look calm and even my heart rate is thumping at a good beat but I still feel the build up at the back of my neck and behind my eyes. My blood seems to move a little more quickly than normal as I rapidly flash different scenarios in my head. Why did I get so stressed out? I forgot to reset the odometer when I filled up my gas tank or I didn't leave the house exactly at 0700 in order to be half an hour early at school. Frivolous things take a toll on me, and when I get all worked up, throwing around some weights is a great release.

Ah yes, nothing is more satisfying than staring at myself in the mirror as I pick things up and put them down. Weightlifting has been a huge help in releasing some of that anger and rage. On particularly angry days, I like to really challenge myself and just beat the shit out of my body with weights. To feel the pain and stretch of muscles being torn is a sort of masochistic high for me that directs my attention away from being angry or stressed out. Add some heavy metal or rock (not that alternative bullshit) like Korn, System of A Down, Disturbed, or Five Finger Death punch and I just go ham on them weights. BEAST MODE, motherfuckers! I start to feel the anger become energy that builds from within me as my muscles begin to bulge with every lift and pump, electricity darts all around me, a whirlwind begins to circulate at my center, and the ground begins to shake and shatter as a glowing yellow light begins to emanate from all around me, my hair flashing from black to gold as the energy pulsates outwards. Every gym rat and "new year, new me" stares in absolute terror and confusion as I surpass level 9,000! Then it happens—I let out a raging howl from my lungs, a nuclear explosion of energy erupts, and I am left in the center of a decimated gym, glowing gold as I achieved a new level of strength. Fools, this isn't even my final form.

At the other end of the physical fitness spectrum. We have much more tranquil and docile forms of exercise that do just the opposite of fighting fire with fire. As much as I enjoy lifting bars of iron and steel, I've also learned to have a balance in my workout regimen that does just as much, if not more, for my emotional and mental wellbeing. Stretching before exercise is a must. Not only can it help prevent injuries and soreness, it gives you moments of reflection and calmness. During my stretches, I concentrate on breathing and emptiness. I attempt to empty out my mind and transform myself into an empty vessel, only focusing on stretching and breathing. Soft melodic music helps me focus on this. Along with my stretches, I perform box breathing, which I learned from my therapist. Box breathing is a technique that helps control the circulation of your blood, reducing oxygen intake and giving you a sense of a euphoric high that calms you. The form is like this: Inhale through your nose, all the air that you possibly can, hold your breath for four seconds, then gently release all of the air, through your mouth. Every last bit of breath of air should be released until you can't squeeze out any more. Hold your breath again for another four seconds. Inhale all that air again and repeat the process. I do this for about three to four times, more if I'm focused more on stretching than working out, but you should do as many as you feel necessary to get to a calm state of being.

Along with stretching, my wife has brought me to Yoga a few times, and it's a bit harder than I thought. Yoga takes a lot of discipline, core work, and balance. While doing Yoga, you also find yourself meditating and focusing on breathing. Sometimes the instructor will speak certain mantras or have spiritual-based discussions. I'm not sure that part works for me so much, but for others, it seems very effective.

As you can see, I practice two very different styles and levels of exercise. Why? You have to have some balance. You can't expect to be cool, calm, and collected if all you do is have whey-protein-fueled lifting sessions with your bros as you scream, grunt, and slap each other's asses after a set. On the other hand, the world doesn't run on flowers and pixie dust, and you need to have some backbone to push through life. Adding a variety of workouts that create a balance is essential to bringing harmony to your spirit and mind.

To be honest, I wasn't all that crazy about hippie bullshit until I met my wife. I'm still not that crazy about hippie bullshit, but I've learned that some of it actually works. I consider my wife a bit of a "bruja" (witch) because she does some of her own sorcery. At first I just thought it was some hippie shit she picked up along the way on her travels, but once I started to look past it and tried to understand why she does some of the things she does, I began to open myself up to it. At times after a stressful day at work, she'll come home with a poor attitude and she can be short with me. I don't get all that bent out of shape, I know I'm worse when I'm moody. When my wife gets in this kind of mood, she'll burn some sage in our bedroom and wave the smoke around the room so that the aroma is strong and can be smelled throughout the apartment. Burning sage is actually familiar to me, culturally at least, but I never really saw family members burning it in the home. The smell of burnt sage is calming and has a particular smell that is fragrant but not overpowering. My wife also does it for good vibes, or good "juju" as I call it—a cleansing ritual, if you will. It tends to work. She's more relaxed and gives herself space to decompress, although, there are maybe times where I come back to a home filled with the smell of burning sage and a sudden fear comes over me—I begin to wonder, "What did I do and how bad did I fuck up?"

Along with my wife's brujeria (witchcraft), she's dragged me along to self-motivating seminars where it's all about empowerment and a can-do attitude. It was full of a lot of flowery speeches about self-love and believing in yourself. I don't buy it, but I have to admit, it resonates with a lot of the attendees. I have a lot of self-motivation and confidence. At times I'm too confident and come off as a cocky asshole, but hey, if that's the price I have to pay, so be it. I wasn't very open to the speakers, but there was one I really enjoyed. Dr. Sean Stephenson was very entertaining to hear and had a great presentation. He didn't have any hippie bullshit in his speeches, he was more of a storyteller and had great stories to tell. He was crass and relatable and had the "I don't give a shit what anybody else thinks of me" attitude. Maybe that's why I actually listened to him. However, with speeches, motivation, or hippie bullshit, you need to know your audience, and you, the audience member, need to know what works and doesn't work for you. You won't know what works unless you give it a shot.

For instance, my wife took me to a sound bath event. Essentially, a group of people get into a large quiet and dark room and get "bathed" with sounds. It's like nap time, for adults. Some people even get all cuddled up with a blanket, pillow, and mat. During the session, everyone is silent and the facilitator begins to play a variety of instruments that include, gongs, metal singing bowls, tuning forks, and other chimes. The waves of sound radiate throughout the acoustics of the room and bounce back, washing over your body like water. Some people fell asleep and were snoring instantly. Me? I couldn't get into it. I kept jumping from one thought to the next. I was getting distracted by the guy who sounded like he was drowning in his own saliva. Then there was hip hop class that was next door and I could hear the bass drop every two seconds. Needless to say, it wasn't for me, but it seemed to work for others.

Personally, I find more benefit when I meditate alone. For the most part, I practice my breathing techniques and meditate when I stretch at the gym before a work out. Another way I really enjoy meditating is in a park on a warm summer day. I go kick off my shoes, let the blades of grass run between my toes, and find a nice comfy spot to sit. When I meditate, I try to think of nothing and just listen to music as I take deep inhales and exhales. For me, specific music is important to help with my meditation. I find myself drawn to the soothing sounds of lo-fi hip hop, a YouTube channel of smooth hip hop beats mixed with jazz instrumentals. I also listen to classical instrumental music, like pianists, cellists, and violinists. What's important for me is that the music is easy-going with a continuous beat and no lyrics. Lyrical music can be distracting for me because I'll start to focus on the words instead of breathing and trying to find tranquility. After 30 minutes to an hour of meditation, I'm very relaxed, refreshed even. I think it's because I take a little bit of time to be by myself, which is actually quite hard for me. I'm an extrovert by nature and love to be around people, it's where I get my energy, but some time alone is good for me too.

Surprisingly, studying helps keep me calm myself too. Sure, I get frustrated when I'm trying to complete a difficult problem, but studying brings a level of focus. The same is true when I edit photos—I can get lost behind the computer, kind of like right now as I type up this chapter. While I'm typing, I'm listening to lo-fi hip hop and waiting to hear from my wife about dinner. She should be finishing up with her hippie bullshit class and she's been craving crappy tacos lately, so I think we'll go binge on Taco Bell or Del Taco. Or maybe we'll just buy a bunch of Jack in the Box tacos. Damn things are addicting.

Hey now, don't go judging me, I did say earlier I wanted to live "semi-healthy". Sure, I eat my greens and salads, and we cook a lot at home too, but that won't stop me from stuffing my face full of pizza and downing pitchers of beer. Like exercise, it's all about balance. During the week, we cook a lot and make our lunches; on the weekends, we indulge, and today happens to be fried taco Friday! My wife has definitely gotten me to eat healthier. For one, I've learned how tasty and filling yogurt and fruit could be. I've also developed a really great recipe for what I call "Zuppa Giovanni," AKA Old Man Soup, which is essentially butternut squash soup.

Food nourishes our bodies and exercise helps our bodies grow and become stronger. Yet, we should not neglect out mental and emotional wellbeing. Now, I'm no guru on top of a mountain who has reached enlightenment. These are just observations that have worked for me. If you think about it, mind, body, and soul are all connected, and if one of these three are out of commission, other areas become affected. Make sure to nurture your mind and heart as well as your body. There's no point in having a drop dead gorgeous bod if you have a weak heart or mind full of agony. Balance is not something that happens overnight, nor does it come easily, but with enough effort and discipline, you too can become your own healing temple.

Cleanliness Is Next To Godliness

When you come out of the military, you soon realize that things are not as they should be. Settling back into civilian life can be rather unnerving because there is a level of expectation that has been ingrained into us by the military. Things don't run like clockwork, and not everyone is as professional as we would like them to be. It's frustrating, but you come to understand that there are some things you can control and others you cannot.

For starters, we can't control other people's perceptions. We may have had lots of influence on our soldiers and counterparts, but that goes out the window when you hang up the uniform. It's frustrating to realize that your words no longer carry any clout. In fact, most people don't give two shits about who you are, unless they find out you're a vet, in which case maybe you'll get a thank you and 10% off your purchase, but beyond that, you're an average nobody just like everyone else. I struggled with this a lot when I came home; it was a real shot to my pride. I reached a point in my military career where soldiers knew who I was and what I had accomplished just by looking at my uniform. I was a Sergeant, I had a 101st Airborne patch on my right shoulder, a Combat Action Badge on my left chest, and a weathered look of experience and war upon my face. There was no question about who I was or what I had accomplished. I was given respect and was counseled for guidance. I was a source of wisdom, structure, and leadership. Soldiers looked up to me and my superiors praised me. No one gave me any more shit details and I was always asked to help instruct the young soldiers as they prepared for their own deployments. It's as if I finally made my mark on life, and as soon as I waved goodbye to the military, it was all swiftly taken away from me. Someone hit the restart button on my game of life and I was starting over with nothing. People viewed me as nothing but another 26 year old kid, my words had lost their impact and no longer mattered, my experience did not matter, my training and education, none of it mattered anymore. I did not matter. I was alone and I was nobody. Welcome to the civilian side.

After a few years of social neglect and realizing that indeed, no one cared about what I did or who I was. It was up to me to recreate myself. I was no longer a soldier; I was still a veteran but being a veteran would only get me so far. I had to do some spiritual healing and cleaning and begin to throw out old habits that no longer served me so I could start implementing new ones that did. I had to learn to be okay with no longer being admired and respected. How are people supposed to judge me if I don't have a uniform that tells my life's story? I'd have to show them by my actions and find a new voice. If I wanted people to change their perception of me, I'd have to adapt to this new world and change—the world doesn't change for me.

For starters, I stopped always referring to the military in conversations. I would stop using such expressions such as, "Well, when I was in the Army..." or "You have no idea what I've been through!" I stopped wearing my bloody, dirty combat boots out in public (unless I intended on getting dirty), or that same damn motto t-shirt; I stopped getting the same high and tight and finally tried different hairstyles. I even started wearing different colored clothing, like pink, lavender, and turquoise. I'd get lots of compliments on these colors as opposed to the same black and dark gray articles of clothing I would wear before.

By changing little bits of who I was, I became more approachable. People wouldn't know I was a veteran until much later. I'd talk about the jobs I held at time, the places I'd traveled to, the people I had met. I wouldn't lead with the military when talking about myself; I wasn't ashamed of my time in service, but rather, that was no longer the focus on my life. I was becoming a new person and there was still a lot left to do before I rediscovered who I was.

A few steps I took to reinvent myself were through education. The great thing about education is that your mind opens up to different ideas, and you become more aware of your surroundings and the people in those surroundings. You develop relationships with those you never would have had you still been in the service. You begin to be less tribal and more open to discourse. You begin to clean out your mental and emotional closets and start to reorganize your ideologies and views. Change is good and it's a great aide in helping you reinvent who you are while not letting go of who you once were.

Along with taking some emotional inventory, physical cleaning can be a great aide too. Here's a question: would your room or home pass inspection right now? If not, I have some suggestions for you. Now, I rather enjoy cleaning my home, doing dishes and laundry, and cleaning the bathroom for a few different reasons. First, I can't stand a mess. If you were in the military, order and cleanliness are a must for a functioning soldier. Now, you no longer have a NCO coming in to do room inspections with a white glove, but that doesn't mean you should live like a pig either. Sometimes, doing some cleaning can help organize your thoughts and emotionally heal you. When I'm about to study, edit photos, or write, it's hard for me to be focused if my workspace is a mess. The mess doesn't necessarily impede my work, but it does cause a distraction. So, in order for me to stay focused on the task at hand, a little tidying up goes a long way. I don't know about you, but when things are disorganized, it becomes very hard to have all my attention in one particular area. It's hard to find balance and peace when your home is in disarray.

Have you ever come home to a very messy and dirty home and with one look became frustrated, stressed, and just plain annoyed to the point that it ruined your day? Instead of tackling the job, did you just lie down in bed or find an exit through your television in hopes that the mess would disappear? What you're doing is not helping. If anything, it's bringing you down and causing more pain. I see it like this—our home is a reflection of ourselves, and if our home is constantly dirty, disorganized, and unkept, we reflect those same values in ourselves. If we don't hold ourselves accountable to keeping a clean home, what makes you think we would be accountable for a clean soul? I'm not saying you have to be a saint, but there is something to be said when you constantly have a shitty attitude and your home is always a disaster. Let me ask you this: are you really happy with the messy state of your home, or the messy state of your life? If not, make a change now and start cleaning. Don't wait on others, lead by example. I get it, you're tired from a long day's work or you don't want clean on your days off. Unless you're traveling on that day off, you can take the time to clean. If you start cleaning, I guarantee that you'll start to feel better. You'll be more at ease, less stressed, and begin to find solace in your home. Happy home, happy life.

My wife and I recently watched a few episodes of *Tidying Up with Marie Kondo*. Marie Kondo describes how in our busy lives we begin to clutter up our homes and our lives. She sets out across the U.S. to help families tidy up their homes and their lives at the same time. One aspect of this show that I really enjoy is that she teaches people how to let go of things. There is a scene with a mother who had all of her clothing piled up on a bed. It was massive, more clothes than my wife and myself combined. Marie asks the mother to pick up an article of clothing and to ask herself, "Does this bring me happiness?" If the answer is yes, you put it aside and keep it. If the answer is no, you thank the item of for its years of usefulness and happiness that it brought you and put it aside to be donated or thrown away. There's a really strong metaphor here.

Imagine, if you held onto everything that has ever happened to you or that has come into your life — the good and the bad, the useful and the useless. Would you have any more room for something good or useful to come into your life? Or would you be like that mother, with a mountain of things piled upon her bed, blocking the way to new doors of happiness. We need to take inventory and let go of things we no longer need in our homes or our lives. It's time to let a few things go.

I've definitely had to let go of a few things in my life. Toxic people, relationships, past experiences, and even my own mistakes. None that stuff would have been helping me today, but had I not let all of it go, I may not have had room for my marriage, education, photography, or writing. I could have very well stayed in the same funk, doing the same thing and getting the same results. I would just be getting by instead of thriving. One thing I've also learned about cleaning is that best time to clean is when I'm angry. When I feel like I've been done wrong, I'm angry with the results of a situation, or I'm just plain pissy, I clean. I'd rather put my energy and anger towards something positive and useful. I get a lot more out of a clean home than an angry Facebook rant. Plus, after I've cleaned, I've calmed down and I'm able to readdress the situation with a more level head. Cleaning buys me time and understanding that I need time to cool off and be alone with my thoughts. It's not just cleaning my home that is relaxing or rewarding, but even cleaning my car or motorcycle.

Whenever I have the time, I really enjoy cleaning my car and motorcycle. I like to get into the details of art—make the chrome shine, keep the glass clear, and give the leather a nice smooth surface. I can already smell the clean leather. I take a lot of pride in my vehicles and like to ensure that they always look their best. At times, I neglect them because I'm busy with work or school, but when I put in the work, they look beautiful. Along with cleaning my car and motorcycle, I like to work on them too. It's a nice distraction and break from everyone and everything else. It also gets my brain working a bit more when I try to figure out why a car makes a noise or won't start. I also like doing basic maintenance myself—making sure I change my oil, spark plugs, air filter, things like that. I've even had to change the radiator on an old BMW I had. I made a huge mess of myself but there was a great sense of pride and accomplishment when I was able to fix the overheating issue. I guess it comes with wanting to fix a problem. At first, you don't know what the problem is. Then, you're able to identify the problem, find the best course of action, and execute. This same step by step process that I used to diagnose and repair vehicle problems is the same I use when dealing with my own personal problems.

Cleaning and working on cars has taught me a lot about dealing with problems and disorganization. They always remind me of a special someone that I developed a strong bond with when I was stationed in Germany, my "Deutsche Oma" (German grandma). I met Oma when I was stationed at LRMC and she took to me like a mother hen takes to her chicks, always making sure I wasn't getting into trouble. She was sweet and full of wisdom and didn't take shit from anyone. Oma used to tell me to think of this old German proverb whenever I would come face to face with a problem: "How do you eat an elephant?" I was puzzled the first time I heard her say this and imagined a huge elephant, on a stick being roasted over an open flame. The answer: "One piece at a time." It's a simple and direct solution that makes all the sense of the world.

So whether you are trying to clean up your home, work, cars, life, or some other seemingly impossible obstacle, you need to remember to take it one piece at a time. Maybe you can't get it all done in one shot, or maybe you can only start with one small piece of the big problem. That's okay, do what you can and little by little you'll be able to conquer anything. It's just like calculus—you need to simplify the equation first before you can tackle the problem.

If you want to make your life a little better and a little happier, start with some simple things that you can control. You can control how you look and how you dress. You can control what parts of your life are relevant and important. You can begin to keep good cleaning habits in your home that will carry over into other aspects of your life. Clean your home, clean your car, the garage; start organizing things and understand that it's okay to let some of it go. Make room in your home and your life for happiness and beauty. Nobody likes to deal with a Debbie Downer or a Sour Sam; be the best you can be and strive to make yourself a happier you, but it all starts with one small step, and it's a very easy one to do. So tonight, tomorrow, or this weekend, dedicate some time to yourself and get to cleaning! Hell, all hands on deck if you have a family, and if you have a messy family, lead by example. Be the change you want to see.

"The objective of cleaning is not just to clean, but to feel happiness living within that environment." – Marie Kondo

Politics

They say there are three things you should never talk about in polite company: religion, politics, and money. This unspoken rule seems to be the norm in most households, I presume, or at least that's what TV shows and movies have taught me. However, that is not the case today. In 2019, politics is all around us. Politics have infiltrated our friendships, families, dinner tables, classrooms, jobs, and above all, our social media. It seems that we can never stop talking about politics these days, and I'm just as guilty as the next guy. However, as bad as it may be to talk about politics, I think it's great that as a country we can have opposing views and healthy discourse about political stances. The major problem that we run into as a country or as veterans is in our approach. A question I propose to you is this: Do you want to have meaningful political discussions in order to learn more about your fellow man? Or do you just want to win an argument?

It's funny to think that I would want to talk about politics here in this book, but politics is unavoidably part of the military and veterans, just like when new kings were crowned, they would host a massive feast with drink and women for their soldiers. As protectors of any kingdom, a good leader knows to ensure the loyalty of their troops, whether that be by paying tribute to the military with food and wine or money and benefits, so the military has been swept into politics since day one.

Just like everyone else, us veterans get caught up in all the political hoopla too. We may be out of the military, but we keep an eye on it from afar like an older brother that comes to visit their younger siblings once they've flown the nest. We get so distracted by the politics that we unknowingly get separated from one another and only see blue and red. It's really sad to see this happen. I've lost friends over political discussions, which seems kind of crazy to imagine, but it's happened. We all have boundaries and when those boundaries are crossed, it seems as if there is no going back.

This brings me to another question: How did we allow this to happen? How did our brothers and sisters of war become our new enemy? How did we forget all that we had endured together and let the old fools of the past dictate how we act and feel? And why the hell are we so impressionable? Come on! We might have been programmed to be soldiers, but we haven't lost the ability to think for ourselves, have we?

In my opinion, one of the biggest factors that has created a divide amongst the brethren of war-battered soldiers is that we have forgotten how to think critically. Nowadays, we let memes do the talking. We let media outlets shape our opinions. We let party talking points argue on our behalf. This doesn't make sense—we've allowed other people to put words in our mouths, without questions, without hesitation. Of course, parties will advocate for economic and social issues that align with your own ideology, but does that mean you will always agree with all of your party's advocacy? Do you blindly trust your party and the direction they are going in? I ask you these questions because I would like to see you think for yourself and not just regurgitate what you saw on someone's timeline or the 10 o'clock news.

I think a lot of us vets have forgotten how to dive deep inside ourselves and question what we truly believe in. It's scary, to be honest, to really search your soul and come to a conclusion about how you really feel. It's easier to let someone or some party represent your thoughts and emotions. It's even easier to hide behind a barrage of Facebook memes that are set to antagonize everyone while you just watch the whole place burn as you grin and eat your popcorn. It's all fun and games until it gets personal, until your loved ones are affected. If you've lost yourself to this pattern of behavior, you need to re-learn to think for yourselves and stop blindly believing or following whatever is projected your way.

Question everything. Question the sources that your information comes from. Question the ideals and philosophy of those distributors of information. Are they biased? Do they lean one way or the other? It's hard to really know what sources to trust these days. Why is that? So many media outlets claim to be unbiased and fair but fall short of that. We have an uptick in satire media outlets that pass themselves off as news organizations and their words are taken as truth. We have webpages and articles that have been specifically created to slander someone or some entity. We're also lazy in our fact finding. We don't make the time to research the information we get, even less if it aligns with our values. I've done this before and have realized that I trusted not so honest "news sources." I think we also sometimes just don't care, as long as we are able to win an argument. We've adopted the ability to call something "fake news" if we don't agree with its stance. Even if said "fake news" is true, we can just ignore it or deflect to another topic. Giving up the ability to critically think and research in order to win an argument seems like a high price to me, but hey, to each their own.

Another question you should be asking yourself in moments of political discourse: Is there an agenda at play? Is this an honest conversation, or is there an attempt to sway the argument into a certain direction to prove a point? I like to think people have political conversations because they are genuinely interested in what others have to say, but that's not always the case. Along with winning an argument, it seems the need to convert people is in the air, much like the people that knock on your door on a Saturday morning asking if you've heard the "good news."

I see the same tactic displayed in political debates. Some people don't really care to hear what you have to say, they just want another member in their congregation add another notch on their belt. The individuals who tend to use this tactic put forth an image of being more thoughtful in their discussions and less aggressive, but in reality they disregard any counter-arguments. Like a lion in the tall grass under the hot African sun, they patiently stalk their pray and wait for the right moment to strike. Once they see an opening, they leap out from behind their camouflage and go straight for the throat. They slam them down on the ground, put all their weight on them as they clench down on the throat of the unsuspecting prey. The prey can no longer resist and is dragged back to the lion's side of the jungle. Just like that, you no longer have a debate, no longer have a meaningful discussion. What you have is someone wearing a smug look while the other begins to question their own beliefs. It was never about having a political discussion, it was about indoctrination.

This part of political dialog confuses me a lot. Why on Earth do we need people to accept our ideas as just? What happened to the good old "agree to disagree"? If they don't believe what you are saying or just think you're full of shit, that's okay. If you are confident in your ideas, opinions, and thoughts, you shouldn't be concerned with having to force those beliefs onto other people. If anything, it weakens your argument. However, if you are genuinely curious as to why someone doesn't agree with you, be direct and ask them—why? Don't demand an explanation that can defeat your argument, but genuinely ask why they see things differently, and once you have heard it, accept it and carry on with yourself. That's the point of conversations, even arguments—for people to hear and be heard. If you don't allow yourself to be heard or hear others out, all you will hear are political talking points. I guess this is easier said than done. I occasionally have a hard time listening to the other side of an argument, especially if I don't agree with the moral principle being argued. Yet, one thing I have learned in school is that when it comes to persuasion and arguments, there are different layers to what persuasion can get passed. My professor of Behavioral Management taught me that there are different zones of influence. It begins with a large circle that contains two smaller circles within—in the center is a small circle where we have the preference zone; from there outward is a medium-sized circle that contains the indifferent zone; outside of this circle and to the edge of the larger circle is a legitimate zone of resistance to, and finally, outside the circles, is the non-influence zone. There is a point in a dialogue where your ideas will differ so much that nothing you say can influence another person, because at that point, you will be trying to change a belief rather than a simple opinion. In other words, you can't convince me the sky is green when I believe it to be blue.

Another thought that comes to mind about the politics of today is the overall ideal of party politics, that tribal mentality or need to belong to something bigger than yourself. Many people take their party affiliation very seriously—so serious to where they refuse to even talk to someone of the opposing party. I've experienced this first hand. I was at an ex-girlfriend's family event and the topic of politics had come up. I listened to what was said, which was mostly frustrations with policies or certain political figure heads. Her family was under the umbrella of one political party and they had assumed I was under the same umbrella. They asked for my agreement on a particular topic, and I whole heartedly disagreed with them. Their jaws dropped and immediately followed up with, "Well aren't you a member of the 'X' party!?" I said I wasn't and explained why I didn't agree with their views, and I could see the disgust in their eyes. They continued their talks without me. I laughed it off, it was no big deal and I got a kick out of their expressions, but it got me to think. They had a very mob-like mentality, and if you didn't think like them or weren't in the same club, you were ostracized and kicked off the island.

Do we really need to be a part of a political group? Why is there such a need to be affiliated? I think it's because people want to feel included. Even if they don't agree with all of their group's policies, they often continue along for the ride because their family and friends are a part of that group. Even some of their co-workers belong to that group, and that may be all they know.

Do me one favor when it comes to politics—don't feel like you have to belong to a particular political party. Please don't join a party just to be one of the guys (or gals). You have your own mind, and it's okay to not be affiliated with any party. Focus on the policies and issues at hand. How do they affect you personally? Will it make a significant impact on the wellbeing of your friends or family? Will you be hindered in some way because of a policy? As much as you should focus on how policies and politics affects you, be aware that policies also affect others that are very different from you in a more negative or positive way.

Finally, do your due diligence when it comes to politics. Research your information, question sources, and fact check information. Don't rely on what everyone else tells you, think for yourself, and honestly debate how you think and feel about a certain subject. Keep an open mind, but be true to your beliefs. It's okay to see things differently and go against the norm if that's what you truly feel. At the end of the day, you are your own person and can have your own opinions. You can even choose to stay out of politics, just don't be ignorant of them.

I hope this chapter has led you to be a bit more mindful of your political discussions and maybe opened your eyes to how you see or participate in politics. If anything, I think there is one thing we can all agree on, and it's that tomorrow is never guaranteed, so don't waste it by arguing politics with loved ones.

From SGT. B-G to Mr. B

I never knew what I wanted to be when I grew up. I still don't know what I want to "be." I've always envied those who knew exactly who they were meant to be and what they were meant to do. How lucky they were to have a path planned out before them. It must have taken a lot off their shoulders to know that every decision they made was leading them to a desired state of being, a certain title, or a way of life. I always wanted that kind of direction but was never able to grab hold of it. Granted, I had influences and suggestions from those closest to me, but nothing ever stuck. I never heard about a job, career, or life goal where I thought, "That's it! I'm going to do that for the rest of my life, now how do I get there?"

There were plenty of careers that sparked my interest (dentist, lawyer, cartoon voice actor) but none that really motivated me to give it my all. As much as I wanted that pathway of life; I understand how difficult and how stressful it can be to have to do everything and anything to not lose sight of your plan. I can also see how if one goal or one particular step is not reached in that long term goal, it can feel like your and ambitions are now over. It must be hard to have all your eggs in one basket and then watch them shatter as they give way to a hole. There goes the fucking omelet.

Although I never knew what I wanted to be as a kid, I did learn one thing—I was good at being a soldier. I was recognized by peers and superiors and was looked to for guidance by my juniors. I had two goals in mind when I joined the army: Make the rank of sergeant, and earn my physical fitness test patch. It might not mean a lot to some, but to me it meant the world. Why? It was a way to prove myself that I had what it takes to lead and to have the physical capacity to be in the military. One of my proudest achievements was when I had Sergeant pinned to my collar. I was very emotional and overcome with pride and joy. It was something I had wanted for so long. I welcomed the glory, the leadership, and all the bullshit that came with the new rank. I would now be in a position to help others, inspire, and take the hits instead of my soldiers. At least, that's what I was hoping for. It was also a very sad day for me as well. I wanted my family to be there to witness this event. I wanted to make my family proud as I stood at attention in front of the battalion. I wanted my mother and father to pin the rank on me, but that didn't happen. My parents were separated and not on good terms, so in order to avoid one another, neither of them went. It was soul crushing to say the least.

I did my eight years in the military and got out. Why did I get out? I was tired of the bullshit, and Afghanistan was the last straw. I was tired of having to put my life on hold every other year or so. I was tired of losing relationships, either back home or meeting amazing people in the military and never seeing them again. I was tired of being away from my family and missing out on important events like my sister's quinceñera or my dad's wedding. I was tired of the incompetent leadership always shitting on the little guys. And I was tired of not getting the recognition I and many other soldiers deserved; it seemed that all the glory goes to the top of the chain. I was ultimately screwed out of going to my warrior leadership course (WLC) to make Staff Sgt. The army retracted my orders to send me to Afghanistan because the guy I replaced had ended up in jail. Then, when I was in Afghanistan and submitted my packet for promotion to Staff Sgt., it was denied because I had not attended WLC. My confusion resembled that of a Jackie Chan WTF meme.

So I left the one job I was good very good at and had time and experience in, to do what exactly? I had no clue, I just wanted to get out and didn't think about what happens afterwards.

So my transition from Sgt. B-G to Mr. B had begun, and it fucking sucked. I had to hit the reset button, shake the Etch a Sketch, put in another quarter, and start from level one again. Everything I had accomplished in the military meant very little to civilian employers, and I think I relied on that experience too much. I don't blame them though, it's nice that they want to give us vets a job, but it's hard to tailor what we did in the military to the positions they need to fill.

Well, like I mentioned a few chapters ago, I took my mom's advice and went to work for a local school district as an instructional aide, working primarily with special needs children that were integrated in the general education classrooms. It was honestly a great help to me at the time. The mornings I would wake up mad at the world would be quickly dispelled by rushing hordes of six year olds yelling, "It's Mr. B!" They would tackle me, one kid holding onto each leg, another desperately trying to climb my back while four others tug at my hands and shirt. This was especially heartfelt on the days I woke up "angry." The kids didn't see my anger or PTSD, they just wanted hugs and acknowledgement from cool Mr. B! This was the first time I would be referred to as Mr. B, and it had a nice ring to it. Plus, it would be cruel and unusual punishment if I made these kids say both my last names (although a few did learn them well) every time they needed me.

Working with kids at that school district was great. I was given the chance to mentor, educate, and set an example for these kids to follow. In public education, a lot of the staff tends to be female, so being male automatically helped me out. It made sense to me—most children spend a lot more time with the women (mothers, sisters, aunts, grandmothers) of their families and less with the male role models. This can be for multiple reasons, like the father is always working, not in the picture, or has passed away. (I'm sure there are other reasons too, but these are the ones I ran into the most.) I filled a kind of surrogate paternal role for these children, and though they may not have had a father figure at home, they knew Mr. B would be there, Monday through Friday.

It was an incredible feeling to be this kind of "part-time" dad to these kids, and I like to think I was well balanced to fill that role. I'm a big kid at heart so I love to play and act like a kid. My wife has a hard time with this, I'm sure. For instance, my special little guy, a student I worked very close with, was wheelchair bound. He loved soccer and always wanted to play when he saw his classmates out on the field. Well, I made sure he played soccer every chance he could. We'd rush the field amongst the fury of children, I'd be pushing his wheelchair as fast as I could to get the ball. We'd cover the ball with the wheel chair so that the kids couldn't take it away, and when we saw an opening to pass or shoot, I'd kick it from underneath the wheelchair like a submarine launching a torpedo. When the ball was passed to us, I'd swing the legs of the wheel chair in order to bounce the ball back to the other teammates. It was unorthodox and probably not the safest way to play, but it made him happy and it was another way for him to be included.

Besides being the big kid, I was also the authority at any given moment. Most kids automatically gave me that authority simply because I was male. I think, for children who spend most of their time around women, they learn what they can and can't get away with; a male might be a bit more unpredictable, especially if you have spent less time around males, so it might be better to just do as you're told. Then you top that off with "Mr. B used to be in the army" and it wasn't hard to get my kids to listen and behave. Now, that didn't always work with other children on the campus, but luckily, school grounds are the perfect place for rumors to be spread.

When it came to lunch time, my three special kids and I would make our way to the cafeteria a few minutes earlier than the rest of the class. This would allow me time to get their lunch trays and help set up their meals and help them accordingly. We'd sit next to the exit of the cafeteria, which was also where students would line up for their lunch. Most kids followed the rules, stayed in line, and didn't goof around, but we always had those exceptions. One time two young boys that were waiting in line were a bit rowdy, being loud and disruptive to the rest of the students. "Would you two boys please stop jumping up and down and get back in line," I called to them. They stopped, glared at me, and muttered something to one another that I couldn't make out. Just as I was about the question them, a little girl behind them said, "You guys need to stop, that's Mr. B and he used to be in the army so I'd watch it if I were you." The dreadful looks on those boys' faces were priceless. They might as well have seen a ghost when they realized that Mr. B used to serve in the military. They probably thought they had just become a target and that their life was on the line. I never had a problem with those two again and the best part about it was that this rumor instilled the discipline for me.

Working with kids came with a lot of perks. I opened their eyes to a whole world they had yet to learn about. Every year the school would have a career day where professionals would come into the classrooms to discuss their careers. The staff would ask if I could give presentations on the army. I was more than happy to do it. I thought I could help educate the students about the military and how it's more than just a *Call of Duty* video game and how the military does more than kill people. Needless to say, I made the presentations very kid friendly, but I also focused on the importance of the military's role in the world when it came to helping the weak. I did use PowerPoint presentations (laughs in Sergeant) to help illustrate the different topics, such as: where I've served, the people I've met, the food I ate (yay MREs) and the tools I've used. I even brought a rucksack full of show and tell items that included some patches, a Kevlar helmet, grenades, claymores and K-bars... Kidding, I'm not that careless! It was mostly uniforms, dog tags, and load bearing equipment (LBE). I did show a lot of pictures, especially of all the kids I met around the world. I think they liked that the best, seeing how kids looked like in Germany, El Salvador, and Afghanistan. I explained how all these kids were very different but just like them. They had their favorite foods, went to school, loved to play sports and different games. I could see the hamster wheels turning as I talked about the different cultures and customs each country had.

After one of these presentations, I packed up my belongings, thanked the class for their time, and started for the door. The recess bell had just rung, and now all the kids would be rushing out along with me. As all the kids exited, a young girl approached me. She told me her parents were from Afghanistan and she started to get a little emotional. I told her how beautiful Afghanistan was and how much I liked the food. She seemed very happy to hear that and I think she was just happy to have met someone who knew a bit about her country. She also thanked me for helping her country. She seemed flustered, like she had so many emotions she wanted to express but couldn't find the words to tell me. I told her "manana," which is "thank you" in Pashto. She smiled an incredible smile and seemed happy to hear me speak her native tongue. She gave me a very warm and heartfelt hug and ran off to play. I think she figured out a way to express what she was feeling.

I can only imagine what that young girl or her parents might have gone through. I wonder what she was thinking when I was showing pictures of Afghanistan and describing the children, food, and country but I'm glad I met her. Meeting her and gaining her acknowledgement helped. I'm not sure how, but it did.

This would be the first time I would experience being called Mr. B, but not the last. Soon enough, I would be leaving the elementary school district to go teach at a private college.

I enjoyed my time at the school district, but just as with anything else in life, things don't always work out. After graduating from community college and receiving my AA in business administration, I applied for the data analyst position at the same school district—and got the job! I was happy to start a new adventure and new challenges, and the pay was substantially more than what I was making. However, it would end up being short lived. A few days shy of passing my six months of probation, I was let go from the position. No explanation, no "Hey, it's not you, it's us"... nothing. Per union rules, I was given my old job back as an instructional assistant. A week or so later I saw that my old job as a data analyst had been removed from the department I had worked in, replaced by a new title with higher educational requirements and a much higher pay scale. I soon realized that I had been keeping the seat warm for somebody else.

I got jaded in a bad way. I wanted out and took to Craigslist to find a new job, which led me to apply and interview for a teaching position at a vocational college. Next thing I knew, I was teaching business administration and medical billing. I'll be honest, I never thought that I would ever be teaching adults, but I was very excited by the opportunity to do so. There were lots of differences and a ton of similarities between teaching children and teaching adults.

For starters, students, regardless of age, look to the instructor as the subject matter expert, their guide to successfully navigating them through the class curriculum and helping them grow to be subject matter experts themselves. I relished the opportunity to help guide and mentor my students. I also wanted to ensure I provided a safe and family-style environment where we could be open and rely on one another. I was very adamant about this because through learning more about my students, I realized that for some this was their escape from the world. I would provide a place where my students could grow, be challenged, and, hopefully, find happiness.

Unfortunately, many of my students have dealt with low paying jobs, unhealthy relationships, gangs, imprisonment, lack of family support, debt, and in my opinion, emotional and psychological trauma. How can I make such a claim about my students' mental and emotional wellbeing? Well, lectures don't stop at grammar and typing. Lessons don't only cover credits and debits, and my students wanted learn more than just HIPAA laws. Many times students would open up to me about their personal lives and what they have endured. I was given the opportunity to become a trusted source of confidence, an advisor, and their personal cheerleader. I wanted to see my students succeed, and if it meant I had to do a bit more than just read from a PowerPoint presentation; I was more than happy to accommodate my students' needs.

As much as I loved helping my students grow and find a new, more productive path in life, it could be overwhelming at times. I felt that I was taking on all of my students' concerns, fears, and heartaches. I absorbed it all from different students, even from students that weren't my own. I didn't mind, really, but it was a lot to balance out, especially with my own emotional and psychological wellbeing. As much as I wanted to help all my students and to listen to all of their pleas for help, I had to learn to take a step back from it all.

During my time teaching adult students, I was lucky enough to teach a few veterans. It was actually a lot of fun when veterans where in my class. For starters, they were very direct and professional. They respected the ranking structure of the classroom, led by example, and were always willing to help out other classmates. They displayed the leadership I'd expect from a veteran and many were in student leadership roles at the college I worked for.

During student breaks, it was always nice to retell old war stories and hear about other veterans' ambitions. I also learned a lot about different veteran benefits from these same veterans. We built a great relationship where we were both able to teach; I wonder if it helped them. Maybe seeing a veteran give a PowerPoint presentation was nostalgic for them. Maybe they'd get a chuckle if I'd ask a student if they were "tracking."

I really hope those veterans make the most of their educational/vocational benefits and accomplish great things in their life. I know how badly some of them struggled to make ends meet and how much they relied on their benefits to get them through the month. As a student myself, I'm extremely grateful for the chance to go back to school. I just want to see people succeed in whatever they choose to do.

Every time I saw one of my students walk across the stage and receive the certificate, I felt a strong sense of pride that I did a good job. I don't take credit for their graduation, mind you, but I'm just happy that I was able to provide them the tools and the accountability to build themselves into a better person. Of course, it hurts when some don't make it. I feel guilty, like I didn't try hard enough or I didn't allow myself to be available more often. It's ironic, I don't want to take credit for their success but will take the hit if they fail. I'm not sure what that means, maybe someone will explain it to me one day.

I have taken a step back from teaching to focus on my own educational goals, but I still keep in contact with a lot of my students through social media. I love to see their success and watch them grow. I still try to be there for my past students with words of encouragement or advice, and I also receive lots of praise and encouragement from my students when I post about my business, successes, and new ventures. It makes me appreciate all the connections I've made with my students over the years. I would like to see the world become a more positive and uplifting place for one another.

Earlier, I said that when I was a kid, I never knew what I wanted to be when I grew up. That's not entirely true. Years ago, when I was helping my mom go through her boxes of knick-knacks in the garage, I found a box with a bunch of drawings and work from my elementary school days. As I looked through the old pieces of paper with my writing and drawings, I tried to remember the kid I used to be and I compared him to the person who I had become. It was night and day. I had changed so much and had forgotten quite a few details too. For instance, I rediscovered why I loved martial arts movies so much. I found a drawing of me dressed in a gi kicking a sand bag and saying " I love kicking the bag in my karate class!" I had no recollection of ever taking martial arts classes. My mom later told me that I did attend them for just a week when I was around six or seven. She mom said they had offered a free week of classes for kids, but that she wasn't able to afford the full course. I guess my mom just wanted to me to at least have that experience, even if she couldn't afford it any further.

As I continued pouring over the papers and drawings of my forgotten childhood, I came across a folded up piece of construction paper. It was a painting I did of myself, dressed as a police officer. At the bottom it read, "Giovanni, the police officer." I had forgotten that when I was in kindergarten, that's what I wanted to be when I grew up. In the painting, I wore a blue uniform with a big yellow star on my chest, black shoes, black sunglasses, a blue hat, and a baton that pretty much looked like a black dildo with a handle. On the back of this masterpiece, it said why I wanted to be a cop: "I want to help people." As a child, I think firefighters and police officers are the closest thing to superheroes, people who are tasked with helping people for their occupation.

I never joined law enforcement and I don't think that I would today, but the goal of helping people must have stuck with me throughout my entire life. Being a soldier, I was able to help and serve my country. Being an educator, I was able to help teach and mentor those in search of it. As a photographer, I have helped people see the beauty in themselves and those they love. As a veteran, I've been able to help vets in need when they need someone to understand. As an author, I hope to help those in search of the words to express what they feel and help others understand what many have gone through.

There are many things that I have not had the chance to do in my life, but I've always had the chance to help those around me. I think sometimes we focus so much on the destination that we don't mind the path we are taking to get to where we want to be. We will have successes and failures, good times and bad, but I encourage you, even when the light begins to dim and the darkness seems to overwhelm you: don't stop, don't give up, never accept defeat. I truly hope that you have been able to find inspiration here. I hope that you have looked inside yourself to find the real you. I hope that you muster up the courage to ask for help, and I hope that you will reach out to help someone in need.

We are still warriors in our own battlefields, but rest assured, no battle is ever fought alone.

See You On The Other Side

Thank you for taking the time to hear me out. Whether you agree with what I have said or not, I hope you were at least able to take something away from this. I hope you have learned about me and what others might have gone through in similar experiences.

A special thanks to Daniel Johnson, my editor, for ensuring that my words flowed together and that readers wouldn't stumble over my grammar and punctuation. Another special thanks to Jennifer Han, my cover artist, for capturing my vision and helping bring to life a symbol that could carry the weight of this story in a single image.

Thank you to all my family, friends, colleagues, fellow veterans, veteran spouses, and above all, to my beautiful wife, Monica, who pushed me to never stop chasing my aspirations. Monica, you continuously encourage me to reinvent myself and dare to do the unimaginable. Thank you for your unwavering support as my wife. I love you with all my heart.

To my readers, I truly hope to hear from you. I encourage you all to write to me and tell me what you think about this book. Has it helped you? Has it given you a new focus and challenges? Did you genuinely enjoy reading this book? Can you relate to my experiences, and do you know anyone who could benefit from reading these words? Please send me an email at: **1angryveteran@gmail.com**

Sincerely,

Giovanni Berdejo-Gallegos

A Civilian's Guide to Military Terms

BDU – Battle dress uniform.

Shark Attack – When a newly recruited soldiers is swarmed by two or more drill sergeants, berated into confusion and submission by highly vocalized commands and hand gestures.

FOB – Forward operating base.

Fobbit – Nickname given to military personnel stationed at a forward operating base.

E-5 – Letter and numerical pay grade identifying army personnel's rank and pay (Sergeant).

E-7 – Letter and numerical pay grade identifying army personnel's rank and pay (Sergeant First Class).

Voluntold – Volunteered for a duty, task, or assignment without consent or consideration.

Reservist – Part-time civilian/soldier who trains one weekend a month and two weeks a year.

CSH – Combat Support Hospital.

Weekend Warrior – Nickname given to those serving in the U.S. Army Reserves.

AT – Annual training that Reservists conduct during their two weeks a year.

Drill – Weekend duty or training for Reservists.

M16 – Military assault rifle used by the United States Military.

Sham-shield – Army Reserve expression to describe junior enlisted soldiers trying to get out of duty and other responsibilities.

Black Hawk – A type of military helicopter used primarily for transport.

AC-130 – A military aircraft used for transportation of soldiers and equipment.

DFAC – Dining facility.

Sandbox – A term used to describe being in Afghanistan, Iraq, or other Middle Eastern countries.

IED – Improvised explosive device. Homemade bombs the enemy used to disable vehicles and kill soldiers.

Full Battle Rattle – When a soldier is ready for battle with weapon, ammunition, helmet, and protective body armor.

Terp – Short for interpreter. How military personnel would address local nationals that would interpret for U.S. military service members.

PT – Military exercise commonly referred to as physical training.

RPG – Rocket-propelled grenade.

VA – The U.S. Department of Veterans Affairs.

TIC – Troops in combat.

MEDRETE – Medical Readiness Training Exercise.

MEDEVAC – Medical evacuation.

ETS – Expiration of term of service. When a soldier fulfills their military contract and is released from military duty.

Triggered – When one is offended or has their feelings hurt to the point of emotional and/or physical outbursts.

Blue Falcon – A buddy fucker who is a supposed friend/comrade whose actions could harm his friends for his own advantage.

Hurry Up and Wait – A military expression used to demonstrate the incompetence of command when military personnel are told to be at a certain place at a certain time and wait an excess amount of time only to be told to return to their previous post because the mission/assignment was canceled.

Tarmac – Blacktop or runway of aircraft, usually where military personnel are staged before loading onto aircrafts for missions.

Jarhead – A U.S. Marine.

War Dog – An experienced soldier.

B-Rations – Canned, packaged, or preserved food that is served in the field. No refrigeration needed.

MRE – Meal Ready to Eat, pre-packaged food that requires no cooking or refrigeration and usually has a shelf life of 10 years.

Knife hand – A common military hand gesture where all five fingers are pointing at an individual (shaped like a knife), where said individual is receiving correction for wrongdoings, failure to comply, or ineptitude.

Jody – A close friend, physical trainer, or confidant that is secretly courting or screwing the significant other of a service member that happens to be overseas.

OEF – Operation Enduring Freedom (2001–2014).

OIF – Operation Iraqi Freedom (2003–2011).

OND – Operation New Dawn (2010–2011).

MOS – Military Occupational Skill (military job).

Sick Call – When service members are injured or ill, they report to the infirmary, commonly known as Sick Call, or "Sick Bay."

Water Buffalo – Typically a 400-gallon water tank left in training fields. Also referred to as any large fixed/mobile item that provides water for service members.

ROTC – Reserve Officer Training Corps.

References

Department of Veterans Affairs, O. O. (2017). *FY2017 VA Disability Compensation and Pension Recipients by County of Residence.* https://www.va.gov/vetdata/report.asp

III, L. S. (2017, December 6). *Number of Homeless vets rises for the first time in seven years.* Retrieved from *Military Times*: https://www.militarytimes.com/veterans/2017/12/06/number-of-homeless-veterans-nationwide-rises-for-first-time-in-seven-years/

Jennifer Bronson, P. E. (2015, December). *Veterans in Prison and Jail, 2011-2012.* Retrieved from www.BJS.gov: https://www.bjs.gov/index.cfm?ty=pbdetail&iid=5479

Lawrence, Q. (2015, December 7). *Defying Stereotypes, Numbers of Incarcerated Veterans in U.S. Drops.* Retrieved from www.npr.org: https://www.npr.org/sections/thetwo-way/2015/12/07/458501774/defying-stereotypes-number-of-incarcerated-veterans-in-u-s-drops

Prisons, F. B. (2018, November 24). *Statistics - Inmate Gender.* Retrieved from www.bop.gov: https://www.bop.gov/about/statistics/statistics_inmate_gender.jsp

Rice, S. (2017, September 05). *Differences Between Military,*

Civilian Life Contribute to Veterans in the U.S. Criminal Justice System. Retrieved from www.munews.missouri.edu: https://munews.missouri.edu/news-releases/2017/0905-differences-between-military-civilian-life-contribute-to-veterans-in-the-u-s-criminal-justice-system/

Veterans, N. C. (2018, January 30). *National Coalition for Homeless Veterans.* Retrieved from http://nchv.org: http://nchv.org/index.php/news/media/background_and_statistics

Made in the USA
Lexington, KY
23 August 2019